TOPCIMA EXPRESS

CIMA

Paper T4
Test of Professional Competence in Management Accounting (TOPCIMA)

BPP
LEARNING MEDIA

Eigth edition Feb 2014

ISBN 9781472707758 (kit)
ISBN 9781472708809 (e-book)

British Library Cataloguing-in-Publication Data

A catalogue record for this book
is available from the British Library

Published by

BPP Learning Media Ltd
BPP House, Aldine Place
London W12 8AA

www.bpp.com/learningmedia

Printed in the United Kingdom by Ricoh
Ricoh House
Ullswater Crescent
Coulsdon
CR5 2HR

Your learning materials, published by
BPP Learning Media Ltd, are printed on
paper obtained from traceable,
sustainable sources.

The contents of this book are intended as a
guide and not professional advice.
Although every effort has been made to
ensure that the contents of this book are
correct at the time of going to press, BPP
Learning Media makes no warranty that
the information in this book is accurate or
complete and accept no liability for any
loss or damage suffered by any person
acting or refraining from acting as a result
of the material in this book.

£40.00

BPP LEARNING MEDIA

CONTENTS

Using TOPCIMA Express

The TOPCIMA exam

The T4 – Part B TOPCIMA exam is unique amongst the CIMA exams because it is a test of skills rather than just a test of knowledge. For that reason a different approach is required.

TOPCIMA EXPRESS contains the three basic elements you will need to pass the TOPCIMA Exam in February or May 2014 (note the February exam is sometimes referred to as the March exam although it is actually being set on 25 February 2014).

Knowledge and analysis of YJ

- Chapter 1 is a reprint of the YJ – Oil and gas industry case Pre-seen followed by a succinct analysis of what you need to know about the company.

Understanding of the exam and how to write your answer

- Chapter 2 tells you how your script will be marked and the best way to ensure you get the marks you need to pass.

Practice in writing the exam and marking your script

- Section B has two Mock Exams. These give you the chance to try dry-runs before the examination. Attempting these against the clock for 3 hours 20 minutes will build essential planning and time-management skills. Section C provides Solutions and Marking Grids. Marking your script against the Marking Grids (based on the ones that CIMA uses for the real TOPCIMA exam) will help you learn where to gain extra marks. Reading the solutions will help deepen your knowledge.

Download additional materials when you need them

Some people like the TOPCIMA examination whilst others find it much more challenging. To help you get extra help BPP Learning Media has developed additional support materials that can be downloaded as you need them. You only have to pay for what you need.

Knowledge and analysis of the YJ – Oil and gas industry case

Industry knowledge gains marks in the exam. Whilst you should do your own research and make your own points too, a briefing document on the oil and gas industry, together with a detailed line by line analysis of the Pre-seen material, can be purchased at: *www.bpp.com*.

Practice in writing the exam and marking your script

As many as six additional Mock Exams, with solutions and marking grids, and all based on the Company YJ Pre-seen can be purchased from: *www.bpp.com*

About the T4 TOPCIMA case

How the exam works

CIMA has made available to you a copy of the Pre-seen material for YJ Ltd. This is reproduced in this TOPCIMA Express kit. Between now and the exam, you must familiarise yourself with this Pre-seen material and the real-world business environment of the oil and gas industry. You need to spend the time analysing the Pre-seen material and developing your skills ready for exam day.

On the exam day itself you receive a single question booklet containing a copy of the Pre-seen but with an additional few pages at the end with some updated material. This is the Unseen material.

The Unseen material will contain up to 6 'twists', ie. things that have happened since the Pre-seen was issued and which pose threats or opportunities for YJ Ltd.

Your role in the exam is that of a management accountant working for YJ Ltd. It is your task to decide which of the twists are important, and advise management on its options and to make recommendations as to what they should do.

The examination is 3 hours long, and you are also given 20 minutes reading time.

Taking TOPCIMA

There are two ways of taking TOPCIMA.

1   On a PC

This is the only way available for the February 2014 sitting. In this approach you sit the exam on computers at an exam centre. You will use Word and Excel. More details are provided later in this introduction.

2   Conventional paper-based exam

You will submit your report on paper in the normal way. This option is available only for the May 2014 sitting. You can also sit the May 2014 exam on a PC.

In the exam room you will be given the following **data**.

(a)   A clean copy of the Pre-seen material

(b)   New Unseen material, between 3 and 4 pages long

(c)   A main answer booklet and a supplementary answer booklet that can be used for planning and appendices (applicable to paper-based exam only)

(d)   Mathematical tables, if required

Requirement

There will be two questions.

*   Question 1(a) will always be a report

*   Question 1(b) will require another form of communication such as slides, email, letter, chart, graph

What does the TOPCIMA exam require you to do?

According to guidance from CIMA:

> The TOPCIMA paper is trying to prepare you for the role of an ACMA. Part of this is the ability to think on your feet, which requires a sound understanding of a variety of business and financial techniques and commercial understanding, as well as the ability to apply this knowledge to new information presented to you. This final test of professional competence is testing just that – your ability to apply your knowledge to the case.

What does this mean?

You must apply strategic management accounting techniques. You are given some data, and you may have to choose which techniques (eg NPV analysis, cash flow forecasting) to use to shed light on a business case. There is no 'syllabus' for TOPCIMA and, in theory, everything you have learnt in your earlier studies can be covered. Keep an eye out for topics from the three Strategic level papers but also for management accounting techniques and theory from earlier levels.

You must make decisions. Sometimes you will have to recommend a course of action, with reasons. Unlike an exam, real business situations require you to make assumptions or make decisions on the basis of inadequate information. You have to come off the fence.

You must support decisions. This means that you must justify, with appropriate reasoning and evidence, the decisions you have made.

T4 TOPCIMA learning aims

CIMA has issued learning aims for the TOPCIMA exam. These correspond to the nine competences of professional accountants outlined by the *International Federation of Accountants (IFAC)*. CIMA is a member of IFAC, so all CIMA members must exhibit these competences. CIMA uses the TOPCIMA exam to test that you have the competences required in qualified accountants.

Aim Students...	Comment
(a) ... have a sound technical knowledge of the specific subjects within the curriculum	If you've passed the other papers you should know enough – but you may have to revise topics from earlier parts of the curriculum. BPP Passcards are great memory joggers. The syllabus for T4 is the whole of the CIMA syllabus.
(b) ... can apply technical knowledge in an analytical and practical manner	You will have had some experience of this, but you must realise that textbook models may oversimplify or require you to make assumptions. Always consider the context of the case.
(c) ... can extract, from various subjects, the knowledge required to solve many-sided or complex problems	T4 covers several disciplines.
(d) ... can solve a particular problem by distinguishing the relevant information from the irrelevant, in a given body of data	In any business situation, there are issues that need attention and those that are less important. These are not always obvious, however. Information may form part of an important argument or can be used as an input to a theoretical model.

Aim Students...	Comment
(e) ... can, in multi-problem situations, identify the problems and prioritise them in the order in which they need to be addressed	Prioritisation – you must put things in an order and explain your rationale, ie why early things are more important than later ones.
(f) ... appreciate that there can be alternative solutions and understand the role of judgement in dealing with them	In any situation, there are a range of alternatives. You should 'identify, evaluate and rank' these alternatives, using the classic tests, perhaps, of: • Suitability (SWOT) • Acceptability (stakeholder) • Feasibility (cost/benefit)
(g) ... can integrate diverse areas of knowledge and skills	A business decision requires the use of a number of different skills, eg words and calculations. These must be integrated in a coherent way.
(h) ... can communicate effectively with users, including formulating realistic recommendations, in a concise and logical fashion	There are two aspects to logic: • The quality of your reasoning, which means that the arguments you put forward should lead to your conclusions • The quality of your communication skills
(i) ... can identify, advise on and/or resolve ethical dilemmas	Ethics covers personal ethics as a management accountant and the ethical stance of the business, corporate governance and social responsibility. Note that social responsibility and ethics are not the same. These issues are not without controversy.

The steps to passing T4 TOPCIMA

The key to success is producing an effective report in the exam room. To do this you must:

- Familiarise yourself with the layout of the Pre-seen material by reading it over frequently. This will help you find facts quickly in the exam.

- Understand the situation of YJ Ltd through ensuring you understand the analysis in Chapter 1 and by adding your own points. You may need to back your points up on exam day.

- Understand the industry by researching the market place, real world companies like YJ Ltd and trends in the economy surrounding them.

- Get plenty of practice writing mock exams against the clock and marking your answers. The two Mock Exams included here provide excellent practice and can be supplemented by the additional mock exams which can be purchased from *www.bpp.com*.

ANALYSING THE PRE-SEEN MATERIAL

1

Activities

- Read the case quickly, twice
- Re-read it again more carefully
- Mark-up the case, taking notes & highlighting key words

BPP Note

- In our notes following, the page references relate to the page of the published CIMA Pre-seen case – not the page number of this BPP Learning Media product.
- The same assessment matrix will be used in the February and May exams.
- Be aware that you are looking to **identify and analyse** the **key points** in the pre-seen, and that **not every paragraph will be a key point.**

You may find it useful to **photocopy** the copy of the preseen you downloaded from CIMA's website, so you can mark up ideas which occur to you.

For this you should:

- Give each paragraph a reference number.
- Highlight or underline key words.
- Note down any ideas that occur to you as you read through the case.

T4 – Part B Case Study Examination

For examinations on Tuesday 25 February 2014 and on Thursday 22 May 2014

PRE-SEEN MATERIAL, PROVIDED IN ADVANCE FOR PREPARATION AND STUDY FOR THE EXAMINATIONS IN MARCH AND MAY 2014
INSTRUCTIONS FOR POTENTIAL CANDIDATES
This booklet contains the pre-seen case material for the above examinations. It will provide you with the contextual information that will help you prepare yourself for the examinations.
The Case Study Assessment Criteria, which your script will be marked against, is included on page 17.
You may not take this copy of the pre-seen material into the examination hall. A fresh copy will be provided on the examination day.
Unseen material will be provided on the examination day; this will comprise further context and the examination question.
The examination will last for three hours. You will be allowed 20 minutes reading time **before the examination begins** during which you should read the question paper and, if you wish, make annotations on the question paper. However, you will **not** be allowed, **under any circumstances**, to either begin writing or using your computer to produce your answer or to use your calculator during the reading time.
You will be required to answer ONE question which may contain more than one element.
For PC examinations only: Your computer will contain two blank files – a Word and an Excel file. Please ensure that you check that the file names for these two documents correspond with your candidate number.

Page

Contents of this booklet:

YJ - Oil and gas industry case

Industry background

1 Oil is a naturally formed liquid found in the Earth's crust and preserved there for many millions of years. Oil is being extracted in increasing volumes and is vital to many industries for maintaining industrial growth and for all forms of transportation. Natural gas is used in a wide variety of industrial processes, for electricity generation, as well as for domestic heating. Natural gas is described as the "cleanest" of all fossil fuels, as it generates the lowest levels of carbon emissions of all of the fossil fuels. The Middle East remains the region of the world which has the largest proven oil reserves, with Saudi Arabia alone possessing over 20% of the known global oil reserves. Additionally, the UK's North Sea and areas in USA, Canada and Russia still have substantial reserves and much oil and gas exploration work is currently being undertaken in, and around the coasts of, Asian and African countries.

2 It is not known how long the world's oil reserves will last. However, the oil industry has stated that there are only 40 years of proven reserves. However, with improved technology, there is expected to be the ability to extract more oil from known reserves. Therefore, the length of time that oil reserves will last is expected to exceed 40 years. However, another factor affecting the life of oil reserves is the speed of consumption. This had been forecast to grow at a higher rate than has actually occurred in recent years. Cutting oil consumption further will prolong the life of global oil reserves.

3 Natural gas reserves are estimated to last for over 60 years at the current global rate of consumption. However, this forecast may be understated as new gas reserves are identified and come into production. These natural gas reserves are based on geological and engineering information on the volumes that can be extracted using existing economic and operating conditions. New natural gas fields are being discovered and with the use of new technology gas reserves are able to enter production in some of the climatically harsher areas of the world, including in the sub-Arctic area. Hydraulic fracturing is a technique used to extract natural gas, including shale gas, from rock layers below ground using pressurised fluids and is widely used in the USA. The rising demand for natural gas from Asia in particular, may push up natural gas prices.

4 Almost all off-shore oil fields also contain reserves of natural gas. Therefore, drilling and production of oil also provides the opportunity to produce and sell natural gas from these reserves.

5 A glossary of terms and definitions is shown on page 12.

6 There are three major sectors in the oil and gas industry and these are:

1. Upstream – this involves the exploration, drilling of exploratory wells, subsequent drilling and production of crude oil and natural gas. This is referred to as the "exploration and production" (E & P) business sector.

2. Midstream – this involves the transportation of oil by tankers around the world and the refining of crude oil. Gas is transported in two ways, either by gas pipeline or by freezing the gas to transform it into a liquid and transporting it in specialised tanker ships. Gas in this form is called Liquefied Natural Gas (LNG).

3. Downstream – this involves distributing the by-products of the refined oil and gas down to the retail level. The by-products include gasoline, diesel and a variety of other products.

7 Most large international oil and gas companies are known as being "integrated" because they combine upstream activities (oil and gas exploration and extraction), midstream (transportation and the refining process) and downstream operations (distribution and retailing of oil and gas products).

8　This case study is concerned _only_ with _upstream operations_ within the oil and gas industry.

9　The oil and gas industry comprises a variety of types of company including the following:

- Operating companies - these hold the exploration and production licences and operate production facilities. Most of these are the large multi-national companies which are household names.

- Drilling companies - these are contracted to undertake specialist drilling work and which own and maintain their own mobile drilling rigs and usually operate globally.

- Major contractors - these are companies which provide outsourced operational and maintenance services to the large operating companies.

- Floating production, storage and offloading vessels (FPSO's) – these companies operate and maintain floating production, storage and offloading facilities and look like ships but are positioned at oil and gas production sites for years at a time.

- Service companies – these outsourcers provide a range of specialist support services including test drilling, divers and even catering services for off-shore drilling facilities.

Licences

10　All companies operating in the exploration and production (E & P) sector need to have a licence to operate each oil and gas field. Each country around the world owns the mineral rights to all gas and oil below ground or under the sea within its territorial waters. The country which owns the mineral rights will wish to take a share in the profits derived from any oil or gas produced. This generates enormous revenues for these mineral rich countries.

11　The government of the country which owns the onshore or off-shore land will issue a licence based on a set of criteria. Any company wishing to operate in the E & P sector needs to prove its credentials to the respective government in terms of:

- its technical ability to bring the potential oil and gas fields into production
- its awareness and track record in respect of environmental issues
- the company's financial capacity in respect of the investment required to bring the oil and gas field into production.

12　When an E & P company has identified by survey work a potential site (but before any drilling has commenced) it needs to apply for a licence. Licensing is conducted in differing ways in different areas of the world and there are a variety of alternative types of licence that can be applied for. An E & P company could simply apply for a licence to drill to identify whether an oil and gas field exists and to establish the size of it before selling the rights to another company to then apply for a production licence. Alternatively an E & P company could apply for a production licence which allows it to drill and take the oil and gas fields into production. Licences can be sold on to other companies but this is subject to approval by the government that had issued the licence.

13　The governments of the countries which have the natural resources of oil and gas raise large amounts of revenue from licensing the right to drill and to bring the oil and gas fields into production. There are several ways in which the government raises funds from licensing, including entering into a joint venture agreement with the oil and gas company to share profits.

14　The most commonly used form of licensing is through a "Production-Sharing Agreement" (PSA) licence. A PSA licence is where the government will take an agreed negotiated percentage share in the profits generated by the production of oil and gas, i.e. revenues from the sale of oil and gas less the amortised cost of drilling, any royalty taxes (see below) and all of the production costs. However, the entire cost and risk of test drilling rests with each E & P company. If no oil or gas is produced, then the entire loss rests with the oil and gas company.

15 The government will only share in the profits when oil and gas is actually produced, and therefore the split of profits usually allows the oil and gas company to have the largest share, but this will vary from government to government and on negotiation skills. Additionally, most governments also impose a "royalty" tax, based on a percentage of the market value of the oil and gas production.

16 Depending on negotiations and the number of E & P companies applying for a licence, the government which owns the oil and gas field is sometimes able to take a large percentage of the profits, often making production of oil and gas uneconomic for the oil and gas company.

17 Success in being awarded a licence will depend on negotiations concerning the split of profits and also in some countries the relationship between the oil and gas company and government officials. Companies bidding for potentially lucrative licences have sometimes made illegal payments to government officials or their representatives to gain favour. It is often difficult to determine whether a particular oil and gas company has been selected due to its competitive bid, its competence, or whether it was due to the relationship with a government official.

18 Some of the smaller E & P companies apply initially for a licence to drill to identify the size of the reserves at the oil and gas field and subsequently sell the proven oil and gas reserves to a larger oil and gas production company which will then need to apply for a production licence before production can commence. However, some E & P companies proceed to apply for a production licence and commence producing oil and gas which they sell on the open market, and share the resultant profits with the licensing government in accordance with its licence.

19 Once an oil and gas field has been test drilled to determine the proven size of oil and gas reserves, production drilling can commence. The time taken from identification of a potential oil and gas field to the start of oil being produced normally varies between one and three years.

20 The total capital investment for drilling undertaken in each licensed gas and oil field that goes into production can reach, or even exceed, US$ 100 million and depends on a number of factors. For example, the cost could exceed US$ 500 million if the oil and gas fields are in deep water locations and many production wells are required.

Independent oil and gas exploration and production (E & P) companies

21 Independent oil and gas E & P companies are an important feature in the liberalised global energy market. The UK and some other European countries have a substantial and growing oil and gas exploration and production business sector which comprises a range of small listed companies. Some are listed on Alternative Investment Markets (AIMs) whereas some others have a full stock exchange listing. The investors are typically large institutional investors which want to see long term growth in share prices as the companies become successful in identifying and bringing new oil and gas fields into production.

22 These small European oil and gas exploration and production companies have almost 200 offshore drilling licences spread across over 50 countries worldwide. These companies play a vital role in the oil and gas exploration and production industry as they have a wide knowledge of the industry and their employees have the expertise and skill base to research and identify possible oil and gas fields and to bring those with the most potential into production.

YJ Ltd

23 YJ Ltd (YJ) is a UK company which became listed on the AIM in January 2007 with an initial public offering (IPO) of US$ 60 million. Its main shareholders are 12 large institutional shareholders which together own 96% of the shares. YJ had been formed two years earlier with the purpose of identifying potential oil and gas fields that could to be brought into production.

24 The principal activity of YJ is the exploration and production of oil and gas fields. The company's strategy is to explore, appraise and develop into production its licensed oil and gas fields both safely and responsibly. Value is created as YJ proceeds through the initial stages of exploration through to production.

25   A summary of YJ's current operations is shown on page 7.

26   To date, YJ has been successful in identifying and bringing into production three oil and gas fields. This involved obtaining the required licences, test drilling and then proceeding through to production drilling at these three locations. It has therefore been successful in achieving its investors' expectations. However, the oil and gas exploration industry is hugely capital intensive before any oil or gas can be brought into production and sold. Therefore, equity funding alone was inadequate to fund YJ's plans. Following the identification of YJ's first two oil and gas fields in 2008, it was successful in securing loans totalling US$ 140 million to help to finance production drilling. These loans are repayable in 2018 and are at an interest rate of 11% per year. It was able to secure this funding after successful test drilling and obtaining licences and obtaining an independent report on the proven oil and gas reserves at these two locations.

27   YJ's bank also provides an overdraft facility of a maximum of US$ 5.0 million to help meet the peak demands in working capital. The overdraft interest rate is 12% per year.

YJ's Board

28   YJ's Board consists of a non-executive Chairman and five non-executive directors as well as six executive directors.

29   A summary of YJ's Board is shown in **Appendix 1** on page 13.

30   The founding Chief Executive Officer (CEO), Oliver Penn had always wanted to form an E & P company and to recruit a team of experts in their specialised areas which he could trust to share his vision of success. He was very pleased with YJ's success since YJ's formation in 2005. However, he suffered serious ill health and chose to retire in October 2013.

31   The newly appointed CEO, Ullan Shah, has spent his first month since starting in December 2013, visiting all of YJ's operational oil and gas fields and speaking to the geologists and survey teams on current potential oil and gas fields. At the first board meeting after Ullan Shah had been appointed, he informed his colleagues that he wants YJ to identify and bring new oil and gas fields into operation at a faster rate than currently achieved. Orit Mynde was concerned that YJ did not currently have adequate funding in place for test and production drilling at new locations. This is because almost all of YJ's cash generated from operations was already being spent on current operational oil and gas fields as well as on surveying potential new oil and gas fields. Further new funding would be required for test and production drilling at any newly licensed oil and gas fields, depending on if, and when, YJ was to be granted further licences.

YJ's shares and financials

32   YJ has 10 million shares in issue, each of US$ 1 par value. The shares were offered at the IPO at US$ 6 per share. This comprised the nominal value of US$ 1 per share plus a share premium of US$ 5 per share. The company has an authorised share capital of 50 million shares. The company has not issued any further shares since its IPO in 2007. However, the new CEO, Ullan Shah, is planning to buy 200,000 shares on the market early in 2014. To date, the Board of YJ has not declared any dividends. The shares are held as follows:

	Number of shares held at 30 September 2013	Percentage shareholding
	Million	
Institutional shareholders	9.60	96.0 %
Oliver Penn (now retired)	0.20	2.0 %
Orit Mynde	0.05	0.5 %
Milo Purdeen	0.10	1.0 %
Jason Oldman	0.05	0.5 %
Total	10.00	100 %

33   Even though YJ is listed in the UK, it prepares its accounts in US Dollars, as is usual in the oil and gas industry. All revenues from the sale of oil and gas are priced in US Dollars. Its operating expenses are incurred in a range of European, African and Asian currencies, and therefore it is exposed to the impact of currency fluctuations. Where possible, YJ uses a range of hedging techniques to minimise its currency exposure.

34   YJ's revenues grew by 47% to US$ 174.0 million in 2012/13 and the company reported record post-tax profits of US$ 41.0 million (2011/12 was US$ 20 million). The company has made operating losses in each year through to and including 2010/11 due to high exploration costs that precede the revenue streams.

35   Its first profitable year was the year ended 30 September 2012 and all of its previous tax losses resulted in no tax being payable for the 2011/12 financial year. The level of profits in the year ended 30 September 2013 were sufficiently high for the remaining tax losses to be used up, resulting in a small tax liability in the last financial year.

36   An extract from YJ's accounts for the year ended 30 September 2013 is shown in **Appendix 2** on page 14.

37   YJ's cash flow statement for the year ended 30 September 2013 is shown in **Appendix 3** on page 15.

Drilling for oil and gas

38   All of the drilling operations that YJ undertakes are off-shore. YJ's geologists and surveys teams are experts at studying and scanning potential areas for oil and gas reserves. YJ's team undertakes extensive survey work over potential oil and gas fields including 2D and 3D seismic surveys and controlled source electromagnetic mapping to try to establish the size and depth of possible oil and gas reserves, before licence applications and test drilling commences.

39   Once a location has been identified and licences obtained, then an off-shore installation is set up. Oil and gas off-shore installations are industrial "towns" at sea, carrying the people and equipment required to access the oil and gas reserves hundreds or even thousands of metres below the seabed. YJ uses outsourced drilling teams and outsourced service personnel for these off-shore installations. YJ hires mobile drilling platforms and FPSOs as the cost of owning drilling platforms is too prohibitive.

40   The cost of drilling each production shallow-water well can be in excess of US$ 30 million. Therefore, before oil and gas production can commence, it is necessary to undertake preliminary test drilling to confirm exactly where the oil or gas reserves are and the size of the reserves. After test drilling has been undertaken, the most effective way to extract the oil and gas and bring them to the surface is established.

41   Oil and gas fields can be classified according to the reasons for drilling and the type of well that is established, as follows:

- "Test" or "Exploration wells" are defined as wells which are drilled purely for information gathering purposes in a new area to establish whether survey information has accurately identified a potential new oil and gas reserve. Test wells are also used to assess the characteristics of a proven oil or gas reserve, in order to establish how best to bring the oil and gas into production.

- "Production wells" are defined as wells which are drilled primarily for the production of oil or gas, once the oil or gas reserve has been assessed and the size of the oil or gas reserve proved and the safest and most effective method for getting the gas or oil to the surface has been determined.

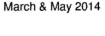

YJ's current operations

42   YJ currently has three oil and gas fields in production. These three oil and gas fields are relatively small compared to some of the larger oil and gas fields operated by the multi-national oil companies. All three oil and gas fields are located off-shore with shallow-water drilling wells. One of YJ's oil and gas fields is located off-shore around Africa, field AAA, and two are located off-shore around Asia, fields BBB and CCC. Of these three oil and gas fields, which had been identified and surveyed in the company's first few years of operation, two have been in production since 2011 and CCC was brought into production in early October 2012.

43   YJ has PSA licences from each of the governments for these three oil and gas fields whereby the governments receive a share of the profits after royalties and production costs. The royalty and licence costs are included in the cost of sales in the Profit or Loss Statement.

44   YJ's three current oil and gas fields have been independently checked to verify their proven commercial reserves. These proven commercial oil and gas reserves total:

- Oil: 9.198 mmbbl (mmbbl is defined as "millions of barrels of oil").
- Gas: 12.780 mmbble (mmbble is defined as "millions of barrels of oil equivalent").

45   These reserves <u>exclude</u> "contingent resources" of oil and gas. Contingent resources are defined as oil and gas reserves which are not commercially feasible to extract using current technology.

46   Details of the production of oil and gas from these three oil and gas fields for the last two financial years are shown in **Appendix 4** on page 16.

47   YJ's geologists and survey teams are currently investigating 12 further potential oil and gas fields. This includes four oil and gas fields in Asia and Africa for which YJ has applied for licences to drill. The outcome of the application for these four licences should be known over the next six months. Milo Purdeen and Jason Oldman have worked closely to meet all of the requirements of the licence applications for the four identified potential oil and gas fields. However, they both find dealing with some members of the government of the African and Asian countries, which own the on-shore and off-shore land, difficult and at times ethically challenging. Some of these Asian and African government officials have requested payment of fees, which Jason Oldman considers to be bribes. He has clearly stated that this is not how YJ conducts business and took a clear ethical stance with the support of Oliver Penn.

48   The remaining eight potential oil and gas fields, in Asia and Africa, are at earlier stages of survey work and exploration.

49   Since YJ was listed on the AIM in 2007, it has applied for a total of eight licences for drilling, including the four it is awaiting to hear whether it will be given a licence for. Three of these oil and gas fields were proven after test drilling and are currently in production (fields AAA, BBB and CCC).

50   Only one potential oil and gas field, DDD, was established to be far smaller than had been originally estimated and was not considered economic to take into production. The total cost of test drilling for the oil and gas field, DDD, which was not taken into production, was written off in the Profit or Loss Statement in 2010/11. This write-off cost was US$ 15.0 million. YJ's geologists and survey team have become even more careful when identifying potential new oil and gas fields following this write-off. However, the fact that only one of YJ's potential oil and gas fields did not go into production is considered to be an acceptable risk, as some competitors incur a higher proportion of write-offs to the number of oil and gas fields that enter production.

51   YJ outsources all of its drilling work to specialised companies. At the end of September 2013, it employed fewer than 200 employees. Of these employees, around half of them work on the exploration of potential new oil and gas fields. Of the remaining employees of YJ, there is a small specialised team which works on licence applications and the rest are involved with the management and supervision of operations at YJ's three current operational oil and gas fields, which use specialist outsourced contractors.

Investors' expectations

52   Overall YJ's institutional investors are pleased with YJ's ability to bring the three oil and gas fields into production and to see that revenues are now being generated, after experiencing over five years of losses, which was to be expected for a start-up E & P company. The market was dismayed at the write-off of drilling costs for the oil and gas field DDD, but one failed oil and gas field is deemed to be an acceptable risk in this sector. Indeed, other E & P companies have experienced a higher proportion of write-off's compared to oil and gas fields brought into production. Therefore, YJ's geologists and survey teams are considered to be doing their research work extremely well.

53   YJ's share price was US$ 6.00 per share when it was listed in 2007, and rose shortly after listing to around US$ 7.00 per share. The share price did not move materially until YJ announced finding its first two potential oil and gas fields in 2008. YJ's share price has fluctuated during 2013, due to Oliver Penn's much publicised illness and concerns over the company's future, but rallied after the appointment of Ullan Shah.

54   YJ's share price at the end of December 2013 was US$ 26.80 per share.

55   Investors are satisfied with YJ's proven reserves and a NPV valuation of its reserves is not required.

56   YJ's institutional investors are hoping for an announcement on whether it will be successful in being granted licences in the four potential oil and gas fields in which it has applied for licences. Other E & P companies have also applied for licences for these four oil and gas fields.

Accounting for revenues and costs

57   The financial accounting principles in the oil and gas industry are complex and the basic principles are outlined below. *No investigation into financial accounting principles is required.*

58   Revenues are accounted for at the point of sale which occurs at the same time as the legal transfer of ownership. This typically occurs when the contracted volumes of oil and gas are delivered to the port in the country agreed in the contract of sale. Therefore, YJ is generally responsible for the transportation of the oil and gas from the oil or gas fields to the entry port in the agreed country, which is usually a port close to the respective oil and gas fields. YJ's customers are then responsible for the onward transportation, or storage of the gas or oil, from the agreed port. LNG is often stored in huge LNG storage tanks that are located near to several ports before onwards transportation.

59   YJ sells its oil and gas:

- at the spot price on the open market to a range of buyers
or
- on a commodity exchange, where oil and gas is sold in the form of a derivative, which is a promise to deliver a certain amount of oil or gas on a certain date at a specified place for a certain price.

60   YJ can always sell its oil and gas production, and it is usually sold before the oil and gas is shipped ashore. The cost of oil and gas production is charged to the Profit or Loss Statement to match the volumes sold. Cost of sales includes the operating costs associated with operating each of the wells undertaking the extraction of oil and gas (after drilling has been completed) from the wells. These oil and gas production costs include royalties, PSA licence costs, the costs of delivering oil and gas to the ports at which the customers take delivery, as well as the amortisation of test and production drilling costs.

61   Administrative expenses include health, safety and environmental management costs, and are charged to the Profit or Loss Statement on an accruals basis relating to the time period to which they relate.

Accounting for oil and gas exploration costs

62   The accounting method used by YJ to account for oil and gas exploration costs is to capitalise all costs of exploration that lead to the successful generation of oil and gas fields. The GAAP accounting concept is that the oil and gas exploration costs are assets that are to be charged against revenues in the Profit or Loss Statement as the assets, i.e. the oil and gas fields, are used. The oil and gas fields are treated in the Statement of Financial Position as long-term assets. This is because, like other capital equipment, the oil and gas reserves are considered to be long-term productive assets.

63   All of the drilling and exploration costs associated with oil and gas fields that are unsuccessful and will not go into production are written off in their entirety, including any costs previously capitalised, at the point that the oil and gas field is determined not to be productive.

64   YJ has capitalised the costs of the drilling of all its wells within its three operational oil and gas fields and this is written off against revenues each year. The net book value of capitalised drilling and explorations costs, together with a small amount of other non-current assets, was US$ 189.0 million at the end of September 2013.

IT systems

65   When YJ was established in 2005 it implemented a range of IT systems using licensed off-the-shelf IT packages. Where possible the industry leading software package was selected. The IT systems are fully integrated and enable the production of executive summary reports as well as the ability to drill down to gain specific data on each entry or event. The range of IT systems that YJ operates is as follows:

- A multi-currency nominal ledger, with integrated sales and purchase ledgers. Each entry identifies the project and the designated areas within each of the oil and gas fields. Therefore, costs can be identified by cost type as well as by each area within a survey area, test drilling location or an operational oil and gas field.

- A fixed assets register.

- Survey and scanning software packages, enabling the geologists to share data and build up 3D images for each area within a potential oil and gas field.

- Health, safety and environmental (HSE) IT systems to monitor and report on all HSE preventative actions taken and all actual incidents that occur. These systems enable all of YJ's managers to extract reports on risk management and preventative actions that have been taken, or are planned for the future.

- Production of Environmental Impact Statements for each location that YJ is operating in, including potential oil and gas fields, as well as all test drilling locations and the three oil and gas fields that are currently in production.

Health, Safety and Environmental issues

66   Health, Safety and Environmental (HSE) issues are firmly placed at the top of YJ's objectives. YJ wishes to ensure that it actively prepares for and manages the risks it faces in the hostile and difficult environments in which it operates. Lee Wang, Director of Health, Safety and Environment, considers that accident prevention is a key factor in the oil and gas industry, as the results of even a minor accident can be significant or even catastrophic. Undertaking survey and test drilling in unknown areas, particularly off-shore drilling, carries risks. All of YJ's survey and drilling work undertaken in the last seven years has been completed without any HSE incidents. Lee Wang endeavours to maintain high standards of HSE in YJ and this has been achieved in the following ways:

- Strong leadership and clearly defined responsibilities and accountabilities for HSE throughout YJ and its outsourced suppliers.
- Appointment of competent employees to manage activities.
- Developing specific HSE plans for each potential oil and gas field which has differing local and environmental conditions.
- Selecting, appointing and effectively managing competent outsourced contractors.
- Preparing and testing response plans to ensure that any incident can be quickly and efficiently controlled, reported on and actions taken to ensure that it does not re-occur.
- Continuous improvement of HSE performance by monitoring, reporting and on-site audits.
- Regular management reviews of YJ's HSE IT systems to ensure that its IT systems meet or exceed international standards.

67 Following some international terrorist incidents in early 2013, Lee Wang persuaded the Board to appoint an international security company. This security company provides trained personnel to improve the security at all of YJ's test drilling and production drilling locations and has done so since April 2013. This security company also escorts all of YJ's employees and outsourced personnel whilst they are travelling to, and from, all of YJ's drilling sites.

Corporate social responsibility

68 Corporate social responsibility (CSR) is central to the way in which YJ operates. In order to satisfy all of its shareholders and stakeholders, YJ always considers the implications of its actions and CSR is incorporated into its management systems and procedures.

69 YJ defines its CSR policies and procedures against international best practice and it covers five key areas. This is shown in the diagram below:

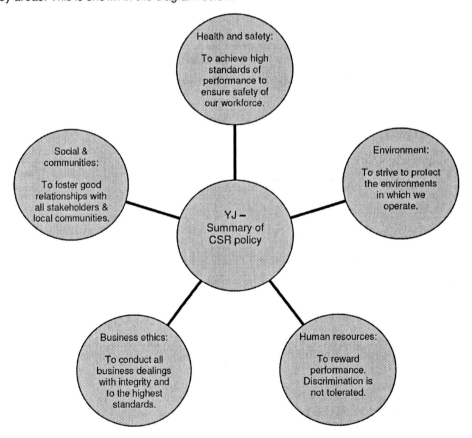

Business challenges facing YJ

70 Like other companies in the oil and gas industry, whether large or small, YJ faces a range of challenges which are summarised as follows:

1. Sustainability issues.
2. Complying with increasingly complex regulatory and reporting requirements.
3. Improving operational performance.
4. Managing risks including financial, political and operational risks.
5. Recruiting and retaining a motivated workforce with the required skill set.
6. Risk of oil and gas exploration which results in an unsuccessful oil or gas field that cannot be taken into production.
7. Managing the risk of accidents.
8. Improving security against possible terrorist activities.

71 The world was horrified by the extent of the oil disaster following the explosion and sinking of the Deepwater Horizon oil and gas drilling rig in April 2010. The explosion was caused by a leakage of high-pressure natural gas which ignited and this resulted in 11 deaths and many injuries to workers on the oil and gas drilling rig. It also caused a massive oil spill, as around 4.9 million barrels of oil leaked into the sea, and this resulted in a major natural disaster that took months to contain.

Farm-in and farm-out possibilities

72 Within the oil and gas industry, companies can buy into an existing licence for E & P or sell their share in an existing licence to another company. The acquiring company has to satisfy the government of the country which issued the licence that it meets all of its specified credentials.

73 These licence possibilities are defined as follows:

*   Farm-in is defined as acquiring an interest in a licence from another E & P company.

*   Farm-out is defined as assigning or selling an interest in a licence to another oil and gas production company.

74 To date, YJ has not participated in either of the farm-in or farm-out possibilities. All three of the oil and gas fields that are currently in operation were identified and discovered and brought into production solely by YJ with no other company involved.

75 YJ had been able to secure adequate financing to enable it to bring the three current oil and gas fields into production. However, YJ has licence applications pending for four new oil and gas fields and is currently surveying eight further potential oil and gas fields. It does not yet have adequate funding in place to satisfy the financing required in order to bring all of these potential oil and gas producing fields into production, assuming that it is granted the licence for them and the test drilling proves that there are sufficient reserves to go into production.

76 YJ will need to either secure additional equity or loan finance in future if it is granted any other licences, or it may be able to use some of its cash generated from operations. Alternatively, YJ may need to consider a farm-out arrangement for part of one or more licences that it may be granted in the future. This is a commonly used arrangement with many smaller E & P companies like YJ.

Glossary of terms

Term / Abbreviation	Definition
E & P	Exploration and production.
LNG	Liquefied Natural Gas. This is where natural gas is frozen to form a liquid to make transportation and storage easier and more compact.
FPSO	Floating production, storage and offloading vessel.
Licence	Government authorisation granted to a company, or companies, for the exploration and production of oil and gas within a specified geographical area (which the country owns) for a specified time period.
PSA	Production-Sharing Agreement. This is a commonly used form of licensing where the government will take an agreed negotiated percentage share in the profits generated from the production of oil and gas.
bopd	Barrels of oil produced per day.
mmbbl	Millions of barrels of oil. This is bopd multiplied by 365 days to calculate annual volumes.
boepd	Barrels of oil equivalent per day. This is natural gas volumes expressed in the equivalent volume of a barrel of oil.
mmbble	Millions of barrels of oil equivalent. This is boepd multiplied by 365 days to calculate annual volumes.
Farm-in	To acquire an interest in a licence from another E & P company.
Farm-out	To assign or sell an interest in a licence to another oil and gas production company.
HSE	Health, safety and environment

BPP
LEARNING MEDIA

YJ's Board

77 *Jeremy Lion - Non-executive Chairman*
Jeremy Lion, aged 50, has been the non-executive Chairman since YJ was formed in 2005. He has held a range of senior roles in the oil and gas exploration industry and he is well respected for his experience, especially in the E & P sector. He began his career as an engineer in oil production and knows and appreciates the risks of the industry.

Chief Executive Officer (CEO): Oliver Penn - recently retired
Ullan Shah - newly appointed
78 Dr Oliver Penn, aged 52, had been the CEO of YJ from its formation in 2005 and he had worked in the oil and gas industry for over 30 years. He was an inspirational leader and YJ's success to date was due to the team he recruited into YJ. However, he suffered very serious ill health in June 2013 and decided to retire in October 2013. He still holds the 200,000 shares in YJ that he purchased when the company was listed in 2007.

79 Ullan Shah, aged 55, was appointed CEO on 1 December 2013, after being head-hunted from another successful, but larger, E & P oil and gas company. He is also known for his ability to bring potential oil and gas fields from survey stage to operation and production in a short time period and he has many important connections in the industry.

80 *Orit Mynde – Chief Financial Officer (CFO)*
Orit Mynde, aged 46, has been the CFO since YJ was formed in 2005. He has worked in a range of industries but prior to joining YJ he was working in a senior finance role for a multi-national oil company. He wanted the challenge of being involved in a start-up E & P business. The speed of YJ's expansion and bringing three oil and gas fields into production within a few years of the company's formation, has more than exceeded his expectations for the company's success. He owns 50,000 shares in YJ which he purchased in 2007.

81 *Milo Purdeen – Director of Exploration*
Milo Purdeen, aged 45, is a geologist who spent 18 years working for one of the large global oil and gas companies in exploration. He has been a keen advocate of the range of new scanning techniques which helps to identify possible oil fields. He joined YJ in 2005 and has been instrumental in the location of oil and gas fields and the successful bidding and licensing of YJ's three current oil and gas fields. He owns 100,000 shares in YJ which he purchased in 2007.

82 *Adebe Ayrinde – Director of Drilling Operations*
Adebe Ayrinde, aged 58, had worked for some large, international energy companies for over 30 years but he became frustrated by these companies' lack of commitment to environmental and safety aspects of drilling operations. He joined YJ four years ago when its first oil field was licensed and ready to be drilled. Adebe Ayrinde is responsible for the selection, appointment and management of all outsourced specialist drilling teams. He does not hold any shares in YJ.

83 *Jason Oldman – Director of Legal Affairs*
Jason Oldman, aged 39, is a qualified lawyer with 12 years experience in the energy sector. He is experienced in negotiating PSA agreements as part of the licensing procedure for potential new oil and gas fields. He has experience in farm-out arrangements in the oil and gas industry. He joined YJ in 2005. He owns 50,000 shares in YJ which he purchased in 2007.

84 *Lee Wang – Director of Health, Safety and Environment*
Lee Wang, aged 48, has worked in the gas and oil industry for over 25 years. He fully understands the enormous risks facing employees, sub-contractors and the environment during the oil exploration phase and the additional risks faced during oil production. He does not hold any shares in YJ.

85 *5 Non-executive directors*
All five non-executive directors have a wealth of experience in the oil and gas exploration and production business and are able to help advise the Board about a wide variety of business challenges.

Extract from YJ's Profit or Loss Statement, Statement of Financial Position and Statement of Changes in Equity

Profit or Loss Statement	Year ended 30 September 2013	Year ended 30 September 2012
	US$ million	US$ million
Revenue	174.0	118.4
Cost of sales	94.4	66.1
Gross profit	79.6	52.3
Distribution costs	0.5	0.3
Administrative expenses	22.1	16.3
Operating profit	57.0	35.7
Finance income	0.1	0.1
Finance expense	15.6	15.8
Profit before tax	41.5	20.0
Tax expense (effective tax rate is 24% but YJ had cumulative tax losses since its formation)	0.5	0
Profit for the period	41.0	20.0

Statement of Financial Position	As at 30 September 2013		As at 30 September 2012	
	US$ million	US$ million	US$ million	US$ million
Non-current assets (net)		189.0		165.8
Current assets				
Inventory	25.0		14.0	
Trade receivables	6.5		3.2	
Deferred tax	0		9.5	
Cash and cash equivalents	13.6		0.2	
Total current assets		45.1		26.9
Total assets		**234.1**		**192.7**
Equity and liabilities				
Equity				
Issued share capital	10.0		10.0	
Share premium	50.0		50.0	
Retained earnings	1.7		(39.3)	
Total Equity		61.7		20.7
Non-current liabilities				
Long term loans		140.0		140.0
Current liabilities				
Bank overdraft	0		3.5	
Trade payables	31.9		28.5	
Tax payable	0.5		0	
Total current liabilities		32.4		32.0
Total equity and liabilities		**234.1**		**192.7**

Note: Paid in share capital represents 10 million shares of US$ 1.00 each at 30 September 2013.

Statement of Changes in Equity For the year ended 30 September 2013	Share capital	Share premium	Retained earnings	Total
	US$ million	US$ million	US$ million	US$ million
Balance at 30 September 2012	10.0	50.0	(39.3)	20.7
Profit	-	-	41.0	41.0
Dividends paid	-	-	0	0
Balance at 30 September 2013	**10.0**	**50.0**	**1.7**	**61.7**

Statement of Cash Flows

	Year ended 30 September 2013	
	US$ million	US$ million
Cash flows from operating activities:		
Profit before taxation (after Finance costs (net))		41.5
Adjustments:		
Depreciation & amortisation of E & P drilling costs	24.0	
Finance costs (net)	15.5	
		39.5
(Increase) / decrease in inventories	(11.0)	
(Increase) / decrease in trade receivables	(3.3)	
(Increase) / decrease in deferred tax asset	9.5	
Increase / (decrease) in trade payables (excluding taxation)	3.4	
		(1.4)
Finance costs (net) paid	(15.5)	
Tax paid	0	
		(15.5)
Cash generated from operating activities		64.1
Cash flows from investing activities:		
Purchase of non-current assets (net) (including capitalised E & P costs)	(47.2)	
Cash used in investing activities		(47.2)
Cash flows from financing activities:		
Dividends paid	0	
Cash flows from financing activities		0
Net increase in cash and cash equivalents		16.9
Cash and cash equivalents at 30 September 2012 (including short-term bank overdraft)		(3.3)
Cash and cash equivalents at 30 September 2013		13.6

YJ's oil and gas production

Operational oil and gas fields:		AAA	BBB	CCC	Total
Location – Continent		Africa	Asia	Asia	
Production in year to 30 September 2012:					
Oil – bopd		1,500	900	0	2,400
- mmbbl		0.55	0.33	0	0.88
Total oil revenues	US$ million	59.7	35.8	0	95.5
Gas - boepd		1,500	1,800	0	3,300
- mmbble		0.55	0.66	0	1.21
Total gas revenues	US$ million	10.4	12.5	0	22.9
Total oil & gas revenues for year ended 30 Sept. 2012 US$ million		70.1	48.3	0	118.4
Production in year to 30 September 2013:					
Oil – bopd		1,500	1,200	800	3,500
- mmbbl		0.55	0.44	0.29	1.28
Total oil revenues	US$ million	60.3	48.2	32.1	140.6
Gas - boepd		1,500	2,000	1,500	5,000
- mmbble		0.55	0.73	0.55	1.83
Total gas revenues	US$ million	10.0	13.4	10.0	33.4
Total oil & gas revenues for year ended 30 Sept. 2013 US$ million		70.3	61.6	42.1	174.0

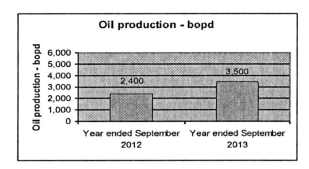

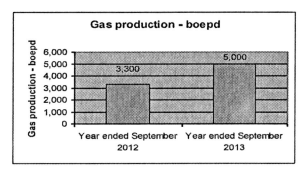

End of Pre-seen material

ASSESSMENT CRITERIA

Your script will be marked against the T4 Part B Case Study Assessment Criteria shown below.

Criterion	Maximum marks available
Analysis of issues (25 marks)	
Technical	5
Application	15
Diversity	5
Strategic choices (35 marks)	
Focus	5
Prioritisation	5
Judgement	20
Ethics	5
Recommendations (40 marks)	
Logic	30
Integration	5
Ethics	5
Total	**100**

KEY POINTS

A key skill in this exam is being able to extract the important information from the data you are given.

Here are some of the key points from the YJ – Oil and Gas industry Pre-seen material:

The strategic situation of YJ

YJ is at risk of being **'stuck in the middle'** in a highly competitive market, and needs to ensure that it finds a viable competitive position, probably based on a differentiation focus strategy based on its understanding of technological issues and/or a regional focus.

The **strengths** of YJ are:

- Good financial record delivering excellent capital growth to shareholders.

- New CEO, Ullan Shah (App 1) track record for bringing oil & gas fields into production quickly

- Track record of success in shallow-water off shore drilling (para 38 & 42)

- 3 functioning fields, good track record of researching successful oil and gas fields (para 52)

- High HSE standards (para 66-67) & possibly CSR (68-69)

- Growing & cash generative (App 2)

- Experienced Board with influence from non executives (App 1)

The **weaknesses** of YJ appear to be more significant:

- New CEO, Ullan Shah (App 1) may have problems settling in

- Concern over ability to finance faster growth (para 11,31) coupled with high existing debt levels (App 2)

- Possibly worsened by its lack of a Main Market listing (para 23)

- Lack of experience in on-shore or deep-water drilling (para 38)

- Lack of focus in terms of its geographical operations (para 42)

The specific **opportunities** facing YJ include:

- Possible opportunities to drill test wells (para 47)

- Farm-out and farm-in opportunities (para 75-76)

- Investment in new scanning techniques (App 1)

-

The **threats** again seem to dominate the opportunities:

- Currency risk, weakening $ (para 33)

- Falling oil and gas prices (para 59)

- Political risk e.g. poor terms offered on PSA licenses (para 14), security threats (para 67), risk of non-compliance (para 70)

- Increasing concern over sustainability issues (para 70-71)

- Accidents / environmental incidents (para 11,70,71)

- Retaining a skilled workforce, especially skilled geologists (para 70)

- Unsuccessful exploration of potential fields (para 70)

The inherent variability of the oil price makes it likely that companies like YJ will find hedging the price of a significant amount of their oil production price attractive, especially given their limited financial reserves meaning that they will find it hard to deal with a downturn in the oil price.

Themes in the Company YJ Pre-seen material

A slower than expected rise in the demand for oil:

The increased availability of natural gas, since 2010, in the US has led to a dramatic fall in its price and this in turn has stimulated a rush to substitute gas for oil in the US and elsewhere. Slower economic growth in emerging markets has also helped to dampen demand.

Security and Heath and Safety concerns:

Oil companies may arouse antagonism from pressure groups like Greenpeace, or from terrorists (in January 2013 40 people were killed in a terrorist attack on the In Amenas gas plant in southeastern Algeria) or pirates (there is greater risk here as Western government have cut the size of their navies).

Outsourcing:

Outsourcing is an established reality in this sector. It would now be very difficult even for major operating companies to dispense with the services being offered by the large established companies that provide these services.

Creating value for shareholders:

YJ's historic losses have impacted its ability to pay dividends. Retained earnings have only become positive as of the year ended Sept 2013. So a dividend payment in 2014 would be legal, but that does not necessarily mean that it would be a sensible commercial move to do this.

EXTRA RESOURCES

A separate and more detailed analysis of the Pre-seen material, the Toolkit, can be purchased from *www.bpp.com*

Practice exams

The two Practice exams in this pack give you a chance to discuss some of these issues. Additional Practice exams, exploring further issues and giving pointers on how to deal with them if they come up, can be purchased from *www.bpp.com*

HOW TO APPROACH THE T4 TOPCIMA EXAM

1 THE ASSESSMENT MATRIX

CIMA marks your TOPCIMA script against the **assessment matrix** shown below. This is a new shortened version of the matrix used in previous TOPCIMA exams. The matrix in your Pre-seen material does not describe the meaning of each of the assessment criteria. The following matrix is based on the matrix printed in the June 2008 edition of Financial Management magazine, and is amended for subsequent developments in the exam.

Analysis of issues		
Technical	Use relevant theoretical techniques and frameworks and perform relevant calculations to help you to analyse the case material and support your arguments.	5
Application	Use the techniques, frameworks and calculations you have produced to support your analysis of the issues and your choices of actions.	15
Diversity	Display knowledge of relevant real life situations within the same or a similar context as that in which the case is set. Additionally, display knowledge of real life commercial or organisational issues relevant to the situation in the case. These may occur in the industry or organisational setting in which the case is set or in different industries or settings.	5
		25

Strategic choices		
Focus	Select the issues you feel to be the most important and make sure that you properly address these issues in the report you produce.	5
Prioritisation	Rank the key issues, stating clearly and concisely your rationale to justify your ranking.	5
	Issues should be given high priority primarily because of their impact on the organisation in the case. Their urgency may also be a factor. Also, state the issues that you feel deserve a lower priority ranking and give your reasons.	
Judgement	Exercise commercial and professional judgement to discuss the key issues. Discuss the impact the priority issues have on the organisation. Discuss alternative courses of action, with reasons, that the organisation could take to resolve these issues. Your analysis should include relevant supporting financial analysis.	20
Ethics	Using your judgement, highlight and analyse the ethical issues in the case and state why you consider these issues to have ethical implications. Discuss alternative courses of action that the organisation could take to resolve the issues.	5
		35

2: How to approach the T4 TOPCIMA exam

BPP
LEARNING MEDIA

Recommendations		
Logic	Make clear, well justified recommendations for each of the prioritised issues and ensure the reasoning for the recommended courses of action is clearly stated. The recommendations should follow on logically from the weight of the arguments and choices of actions given earlier in the report. (20)	30
	Communicate effectively with users in an additional written communication such as draft slides, an email, a letter (10)	
Integration	These marks are awarded holistically according to the overall quality and functionality of your report.	5
Ethics	Make clear, well justified recommendations for each of the ethical issues and ensure the reasoning for the recommended courses of action is clearly stated. The recommendations should follow on logically from the weight of the arguments you make in your report.	5
		40
		100

1.1 Getting marks under each criterion

Technical (5 marks available)

Technical marks are gained in the **Appendices** to your report.

Marks are given for relevant theory that analyses the situation and supports recommendations.

- 1 mark per piece of theory cited which is directly relevant to the case
- Additional marks under the 'Application' criterion are available for applying the theory to the situation the firm faces

Theories that get marks include:

- SWOT analysis
- Strategic option evaluation (suitability, acceptability and feasibility)
- PEST analysis (Political, Economic, Social, Technological)
- Porter's generic strategies (Cost Leadership, Differentiation, Focus)
- Industry life cycle (Introductory, Growth, Shakeout, Mature, Decline)
- Ansoff's growth vector matrix (Market Penetration, Product Development, Market Development, Diversification)
- Mendelow's stakeholder mapping matrix (power/interest)
- The balanced scorecard (Financial, Customer, Business Process, Innovation and Learning)
- BCG matrix

- Value chains

- Product lifecycles and portfolios

- Lewin's 3 stage ice cube model of change management

- Lewin's Force field analysis

- MacFarlan and McKenney's strategic grid

- Peppard's application portfolio

- Porter/Miller information intensity analysis

TOP TIPS

In the Appendices to your report.

- Present one or two technical theories as Appendices to your report

- A SWOT analysis must always appear as Appendix 1

- Further appendices may include PEST, Ansoff Matrix or Mendelow

- You should show the application of the theories in the Appendix (eg illustrate the business options on the Ansoff matrix or put the names of the stakeholders into the Mendelow matrix)

- Include references to other theories in the body of the main report to gain extra marks. Ensure you underline them

- Try to have two further appendices of numerical analysis of issues in the Unseen material

Application (15 marks)

These marks are gained in the **Appendices** and in **Section 4** of your report.

Marks are given for:

- **Applying relevant technical theories** like SWOT and others above to shed light on the case
- Conducting **financial analysis** of issues in the case

The amount of financial computations varies from exam to exam but the maximum has been about **20 minutes** work and **15 marks**. It can involve:

- Calculation of NPV of projects

- Updating a cash flow or profit forecast

- Cost analysis or re-stating product or customer profitability based on revised allocations of overhead costs

- Preparing or commenting on a business valuation

- A make or buy decision

- Ratios to support analysis or a recommendation

You may need to point out the weaknesses or limitations of the techniques that you apply.

TOP TIPS

- Ensure the SWOT includes the material in the Unseen and contains all the threats and opportunities from the Unseen. A common cause of lost marks is candidates reproducing a SWOT based on Pre-seen material and failing to mention issues in the Unseen

- Ensure you apply a second technical theory from the Appendix either in the Appendix itself (with the main body of the report highlighting what's in the appendix), or by clear reference to it in the main body of the report

- Aim to complete two numerical exercises, with most time spent on the calculations needed to discuss the key priority issues in the Unseen

- Ensure you discuss the implications of the calculations in Section 4 of your report

Diversity (5 marks)

Diversity marks are awarded throughout your report for bringing in **real-life examples.**

These can include:

- Knowledge of legislation or other factors affecting the industry featured in the Pre-seen
- Illustration of issues by reference to real-world firms in the same industry
- Discussion of general business issues by reference to other firms

Doing industry research will help improve your commercial grasp and using good industry examples will improve the commercial robustness of your report.

TOP TIPS

In your report you should:

- Provide the names and relevance of at least **three real-world rivals** or other firms
- Mention at least **two specific industry issues**
- Use the **Introduction** to make reference to examples (see solutions to Practice Exams)

But simply mentioning the names of real-world firms and products or projects in the introduction will get very limited marks. You need to relate the real-world examples to the problems facing the firm given in the Unseen information on exam day.

Focus (5 marks)

These marks are awarded in **Section 3** of your report for identifying the issues in the Unseen material.

The Unseen material will contain up to **six problems or 'twists'** that have come to light since the Pre-seen.

The Focus marks are given as additional marks to reward good analysis and recommendations on the main four commercial issues in the unseen material. The marks are allocated to a maximum of 1 mark per commercial issue, but weighted so that a good discussion of 4 issues will gain 5 Focus marks.

TOP TIPS

- **Identify the key issues,** ie four issues that matter most. Group the remaining issues as either 'ethical issues' in Section 5 or as 'other issues' at the end of Section 3

- Ensure you **concentrate on only these 4 issues**, and leave the remaining issues as 'other issues' and name them but do not discuss them

- Provide a full analysis and a full set of recommendations for each issue

Prioritisation (5 marks)

These marks are awarded for **Section 3** of your report.

They may be given for getting management to see what's important and explaining why it's important.

However it is possible that your line manager in the Unseen will initially define priorities rather than you deciding them for yourself.

The description of this criterion states that you should justify your ranking of issues on the basis of their **impact** and **urgency**. Marks will be given for the strength of your arguments and for providing a clear rationale.

An issue can become a priority if:

- You are specifically asked by your superior to report on it

- It is a short-term 'emergency' issue of high potential impact that must be dealt with quickly

- It is something that will affect the strategic outlook for the business, ie its ability to prosper in the future

- It is a broad issue that must be decided before other issues can be dealt with

Some issues may be **ethical issues** such as bribery, safety or corporate social responsibility. These should be **dealt with separately** as discussed below.

There will be different views on what is important and not important. Marking schemes allow for this.

Top Tips

- **Identify four issues that you regard as priority issues** and put the rest as either ethical or as non-priority 'other issues'. A rule of thumb is that the issues with the detailed numerical data will be amongst the priority issues. Another guide is that problems are likely to be of higher priority than potential opportunities

- **List the four key issues** in priority order in Section 3

- Write a **maximum of five sentences per issue** using the following structure for each:

    - **Issue**: A sentence as a paragraph heading, eg '*3.1 Takeover bid – Priority number 1*'

    - **Impact/consequence**: 1-2 sentences eg '*A successful takeover bid would result in control of the company passing to the management of the acquiring company*'

    - **Rationale**: A sentence explaining why the issue has been put before or after other issues, eg '*The takeover is a first priority because the remaining issues would be problems for the new board if the bid was accepted*'

- Keep purely **ethical** issues for **Section 5**

- Explain **why** you have ignored or relegated **non-priority issues** (this usually appears in Section 3.6 at the end of your report)

Judgement (20 marks)

These marks are awarded in **Section 4** of your report.

Marks are awarded for the **'exercise of commercial and professional judgement'** and for **'discussing alternative courses of action'** to deal with them.

The Examiner rewards candidates who provide management with **suggestions on alternative ways to respond** to the priority issues from the Unseen material. You must write a report that **outlines the issues** connected with each alternative response.

Top Tips

- Each key issue should have a **separate numbered paragraph** (1st priority issue as paragraph 4.1, 2nd as 4.2 etc.)

- State **impact** of the issue

    - Evaluate **opportunities** using financial evaluation. Use headings of Suitability, Acceptability, Feasibility

    - Assess **threats** using financial evaluation, outline the impacts/risks, produce a statement of pros and cons

- Identify **at least two alternative ways** of dealing with each key issue

- **No recommendations** on which alternative should be adopted should appear in this section

Ethics (10 marks overall)

Ethics marks are awarded for **Section 5** of your report and cannot be awarded for any other sections.

- Five marks are available for **identifying and explaining** the ethical issues (generally 1 mark for identifying and 1 mark for explaining it)
- Five marks are given for **recommendations** on how to deal with them

Ethics could involve:

- **Personal and professional ethics:** obligations as a Chartered Management Accountant and as a human being
- **Business ethics:** duty to shareholders, duty to other stakeholders, commercial tactics, treatment of employees and responsibility for their safety, and responsibility for impact of business on society at large through pollution, unemployment, or denial of access to essential services
- **Corporate governance:** the quality and behaviour of the Board. It also involves things like the integrity of the management accounting control system, existence of internal controls and the quality of the management and staff
- **Corporate social responsibility:** beyond simply meeting the needs of shareholders to embrace wider social responsibilities. This might involve impact on future generations, responsibility for public safety, need to give opportunities to less-advantaged groups in society
- **Ethical systems:** whether the organisation has adequate systems in place for detection of significant ethical issues and ensuring compliance with internal and external codes of conduct

    It is most likely that there will be 2-3 ethical issues in your exam, although CIMA has indicated that there could only be one.

Candidates lose marks by showing confusion on what is meant by an ethical issue. Ethical issues are not commercial issues (eg it's ethical because it will save some costs or because it would lead to bad publicity). Ethical issues are not the same as legal issues (eg it's unethical because they would be arrested if they were found-out). Ethical issues can usually be described as issues under the following moral principles:

- **Fairness:** this means treating someone as they deserve to be treated or as you would wish to be treated if you were in their position. Therefore discrimination, poor pay, summary dismissal, or refusal of reasonable requests for assistance are unfair. Deliberately distorting competition or taking advantage of a customer's ignorance or desperate position is unfair. Some of these are also illegal, and many would give rise to commercially-damaging publicity. But these things happen because society recognises the practice as ethically wrong and wants to stamp them out.
- **Justice:** this means going through a proper process involving weighing up of the evidence and arguments and coming to a balanced decision and a measured response. Therefore things like sacking someone without hearing what they have to say, or ignoring their side of the story, is unjust. So is punishing someone harshly for a minor wrong, even if the rules lay down that punishment because then the rules and the punishment are both unjust. Justice and Fairness overlap so don't waste time in the exam trying to distinguish them.
- **Honesty and straightforwardness:** this is as basic as telling the truth and not withholding important information or trying to use loopholes to escape responsibilities. It also covers taking assets or value belonging to other people. This principle covers things like corruption, misrepresentation, deliberately misleading wording, and selling someone something unsuitable.
- **Duty, responsibility and integrity:** as a citizen you have duties such as to obey the law, report crime and so on. As an employee you take on other duties that flow from your job and you are paid to do them and put in a position of trust by your superiors or the people that voted you into the post. Therefore you must put personal interest aside and act as the role requires you to do. Any attempt by you to make someone else forget their duty and responsibility, such as by making bribes or threats, is also an unethical action by you too.

Top Tips

- Mention the ethical issues (and ethical aspects of commercial issues) in **Section 3** of your report

- Cover ethical issues in **Section 5** of your report

- **State the issue** (eg dismissal of employee to create a scapegoat) and the **ethical principle** (eg fairness of treatment)

- Discuss the implications of the issue (eg who would be harmed, any trade-off between commercial advantage and ethical behaviour)

- Advise management on **options** the company could pursue and **recommend** a course of action to **resolve** each ethical issue

- Deal with the **commercial and ethical implications** of a problem separately, eg a dangerous fault on a product has commercial implications of loss of production, cost to fix, damage to reputation etc. It also has ethical implications such as endangering peoples' lives if it is not fixed. Deal with the commercial aspects in **Section 4** and the ethical aspects in **Section 5**

- Your report must **not** suggest **unethical** courses of action

Logic (30 marks)

These marks are awarded for **Section 6** at the end of your report. The recommendations should **build logically** from the arguments in your report.

The examiners have said that the Recommendations Section is the most important in the report and this is reflected in the number of marks available for this category.

Requirement (b) of the exam is a further task worth 10 marks. These marks are given within this category for providing an additional written communication in answer to requirement (b) of the Unseen. Marks will be awarded for effective communication. The calculation and discussion will be a summary of the equivalent section in the main report. Therefore the marks are being given mainly for selecting the key points and communicating them clearly.

TOP TIPS

- **Recommendations are placed at the end of the report** in a separate section, not at the end of each sub-section in Section 4 where you discuss the options. They should flow from your earlier analysis

- Recommendations must tell management **what** to do, **why** to do it, **how** to do it and **when** to do it. They should also explain the impact of the actions on the organisation where relevant

- Recommendations **include a justification** of why one option was chosen over another

- For **requirement (b)** in exams in March or September, in which all candidates sit the exam using a PC, the examiner may expect you to **prepare a graph or diagram using Excel**

Integration (5 marks)

Allows markers to use their discretion based on the 'professional feel' and **fitness for purpose of the overall report** and **'the link between discussion of the issues and the recommendations'.**

When writing the report, you will do so as an internal employee of the organisation in the case. This means that the report will need to reflect accepted conventions about your position, and the person to whom you are reporting. Further guidance on this is given below in Section 2.

Key things the examiner looks for are:

- Do **recommendations follow logically** from the analysis of the issues and are they appropriately framed?

- Does the report **make use** of the **technical and numerical analysis** in the appendices?

TOP TIPS

- Demonstrate commercial reasoning and common sense

- Fully describe the pros and cons of the alternative ways of dealing with each key issue

- Ensure each recommendation is justified in terms of how it will address the impact of the issue

- Produce a professionally written and structured document

Your role

In this exam you will take the role of an internal employee who is a qualified management accountant, someone who is engaged in the development of strategic proposals and producing information for the purposes of decision-making. The implications of this are that the examiner will tend to focus more on internal decisions, although you will be expected to alert management to any wider-ranging implications. You may also be submitting your report to a Director, rather than the whole board.

You will also be expected to follow the normal conventions of professional reporting, treating the recipient with respect. However you will also need to take into account your position within the organisation and the position of the person(s) to whom you are reporting. The culture of the organisation may influence your analysis, the recommendations you make and how you frame those recommendations.

When you read the requirement in the exam, you should make a mental note of:

- The role you must adopt
- What you have to do
- The required format of your answer
- Who the recipients are (eg Board, Finance director etc)

To make absolutely sure, use the requirements to head up your report. Here's an example.

Requirement

Hugh Mountolive the Chief Executive Officer can see both sides of the arguments presented by Melissa and Clea regarding closing down the Alexandria factory and moving to Port Said, but is uncertain about how to evaluate such an important issue.

He has asked you, Justine Nessim, the management accountant, to write a report covering all the major factors that need to be considered in relation to the closure and move, with a recommendation.

You can turn this into **a title page,** as follows.

To: Hugh Mountolive, Chief Executive Officer

From: Justine Nessim, management accountant

Date: Re: Analysis and recommendations regarding the proposed closure of the factory in Alexandria and the move to Port Said

---

You have clearly identified the recipient of the report (the managing director), the role you must adopt (management accountant) and what you must do.

3 Question 1(b)

The question requirement will consist of two questions. Question 1(a) will be the requirement to produce the report. Question 1(b) will ask you to submit a shorter item, testing your ability to communicate succinctly to management and present the key points in a logical manner, including appropriate numerical or financial information. You may be asked to produce slides, an email, a letter, notes for a speech, a chart or a graph.

Question 1(b) will always be worth 10 marks. It will be part of the logic section of the matrix. It should take no longer than 18 minutes. It will generally relate to an aspect of the case that is included in the report you produce for Question 1(a). The analysis in Question 1(a) is likely to inform the answer to Question 1(b).

If you are taking the exam on a computer and are asked to produce slides, you will not be permitted to use Powerpoint. The examiner will require you to show what the content of the slides will be.

The guidance below summarises the main features of the types of communication that could appear in your exam.

Briefing notes

These are more informal than a report – but as a rule of thumb, help yourself maintain the overall structure by numbering the paragraphs

Structure	Features
• Heading/title • From/To/Date • Indication of content • Summary of key points/recommendations • Suggested agenda (if addressee is preparing for a meeting) • Main text of document • Concluding paragraph • Appendices	• Informal • Short sentences, short paragraphs • Concise • Not necessarily numbered

Letter

Structure	Features
• Letter heading • Introductory paragraph outlining purpose of the letter and indicating content • Summary of key point/recommendations • References to detailed text in attachments • Concluding paragraph indicating the next action to be taken • Sign off • Attachments/appendices	• Formal address • Unlikely to have paragraph numbering • Report may be attached • Generally for external communication

Slides

These slides could be asked for, or **notes for a presentation**. Again you need to keep track of where you are and to show that your data is organised clearly.

Structure	Features
• Title • Summary • Topic slides in a recognisable sequence • Conclusion plus notes	• Slides themselves should be brief: eg a list of six points • Some slide presentations feature the slides and supporting notes offering more detail

Memo/Email

Structure	Features
• Distribution (To/From/Date) • Special features (eg confidential) • Topic sections (emphasised by paragraph headings) • Emails need to be brief and focus on the main points	• For internal use, and much less formal than a report • A very flexible means of communication – from simple paragraphs to detailed prescriptions (eg instructions) • Should finish with a conclusion or recommendation

Chart/graph

Structure	Features
• As required by the question • Header is purpose of information • Axes/rows/columns clearly labelled • Information presented clearly but fairly	• For internal use to support other analysis • Flexible and easy-to-read • Likely to support other numerical/financial analysis

4 STRUCTURE OF YOUR REPORT

The examiner has recommended the following structure and approach:

PAGE 1

Question 1(a)

Title block

- Who the report is for (eg 'Finance Director of XYZ plc')
- Who has written the report (eg 'Independent Consultant')
- Date
- Title

Table of contents

- Outline the contents of the report in numbered sections. No page numbers needed
- Give titles of Appendices
- Can be used to manage your time by allocating minutes to each section/subsection you plan to include within your report

Few potential marks
- *Integration*
- *Diversity*

PAGE 2

Section 1: Introduction

- 6 to 10 lines introducing background to situation of the organisation. Incorporate Unseen data if it changes the situation
- Avoid explaining or evaluating issues
- Try to include industry awareness examples

Section 2: Terms of reference

- Two lines to set the scene of who you are, who the report was commissioned by and who it is aimed at

PAGE 3 to 4

Section 3: Review and prioritisation of main issues facing the management of the organisation

- Based on SWOT analysis in Appendix 1
- Place top four key issues in priority order with numbered subheadings (eg '3.1 Cash Flow Crisis – Priority 1')
- Justify the sequence of priorities in terms of consequences for organisation
- Less important issues grouped as 'other issues' at end with ethical issues and aspects put into Section 5
- Do not explain the background to the issues nor provide recommendations

Crucial section that carries up to 30% of marks
- *Focus*
- *Prioritisation*
- *Judgement*
- *20% of script length*

Section 4: Discussion of the main issues facing the management of the organisation

Numbered paragraphs each dealing with an issue from Section 3 (eg '4.1 Cash Flow Crisis – Priority 1')

PAGE 5 to 8

- In the same sequence as issues in Section 3
- Explain and evaluate options for dealing with each issue, discussing the potential consequences
- Show less important issues under 'other issues' heading but only write about if time allows
- State main numerical values and reference to Appendix where they can be found (eg 'the maximum amount that should be paid for the new business has been calculated at £3.6bn (Appendix 3 line 7)'
- Refer to technical theories in Appendix (eg 'XYZ plc is following a stuck in the middle strategy – see Appendix 2')
- Avoid putting recommendations here

Important section that carries up to 30% of marks
- Judgement
- Application
- Diversity
- Focus
- Technical
- 40% of script length

Section 5: Ethical issues to be addressed by the management of the organisation

PAGE 9 to 10

- Identify two to three issues and describe why they are ethical issues
- State the ethical principles and duties involved
- Discuss the options the company may have
- Recommend with reasons appropriate action for each

Mini report within a report
- Ethics
10% of marks, majority for recommendations
15% of script length

Section 6: Recommendations

Regarded by the Examiner as *'the most important part of the report'*

PAGE 11 to 13

- Number sections to correspond to each of the numbered sections from section 4. (eg '6.1 Dealing with cash flow crisis')
- In each section state **what decision you recommend**, explain **why you recommend it**, and then **tell management how and when to do it. It should explain the impact upon the organisation** (eg *'This report recommends management rejects the new contract in its present form. The contract is insufficiently profitable and has the following unacceptable impacts on XYZ ......etc. A formal letter should be sent to the management of XYZ Ltd as soon as possible rejecting the contract and stating the areas of concern. This would leave the door open to XYZ Ltd. submitting an improved offer')*
- As a minimum recommendations must be given for each of the prioritised issues identified in Section 3
- Not acceptable to dodge making recommendations on grounds such as 'need more information' or 'firm needs a strategic plan to deal with this'

Most important section worth up to 30% of the marks
- Logic
- Integration
- Judgement
- 25% of script length

Section 7: Conclusion

Brief five lines for closing comments

Very few marks here

Appendices

Put at back of answer booklet/Word document and on Excel spreadsheets

Appendix 1 SWOT analysis, putting issues in order of priority

Appendices 2 and 3 other theory (Mendelow's stakeholder map, Ansoff's matrix, PEST, Porter's generic strategies or 5 Forces)

Appendix 4 etc: numerical workings

Key data and analysis given in Appendices should also be discussed within the body of the report

Essential for justification of analysis and recommendations
- Technical
- Application

Question 1(b)

The separate written item, slides, email, letter, graphs, charts

Clear and appropriate labelling depending on format required

Inclusion of financial/numerical content if required

10 marks

Mock Exam 1

YJ – Unseen material provided for mock exam 1

Additional (Unseen) information relating to the case is given on the following pages.

Read all of the additional material before you answer the question

ANSWER THE FOLLOWING QUESTIONS

The Chief Financial Officer of YJ has asked you, the management accountant, to provide advice and recommendations on the issues facing YJ.

Question 1 part (a)

Prepare a report that prioritises analyses and evaluates the issues facing YJ and makes appropriate recommendations.

(Total marks for question 1a = 90 Marks)

Question 1 part (b)

As an appendix to the main report, prepare an email to Orit Mynde which summarises your evaluation of the 3 potential new oil and gas fields, including any relevant financial information, together with a summary of the rationale to support your recommendation.

(Total marks for question 1b = 10 Marks)

Your script will be marked against the T4 Part b Case Study Assessment Criteria shown below:

Analysis of Issues	25
Technical	5
Application	15
Diversity	5

Strategic Choices	35
Focus	5
Prioritisation	5
Judgement	20
Ethics	5
Recommendations	40
Logic	30
Integration	5
Ethics	5

Read this information before you answer the question

New oil and gas fields

When Ullan Shah joined YJ he immediately informed his colleagues on the Board and the institutional investors that YJ would identify and bring into production oil and gas fields at a much faster rate than it had done to date. He is critical of YJ's overly risk averse approach to growth and development and has pledged to sharply increase YJ's output, revenues and ultimately the share price over the next 3 years.

One of his first actions, in the first two weeks of joining, was speak to the geologists and survey teams to find out which of the 12 potential oil and gas fields YJ is investigating could be brought into production in the next 12 months.

Shah has received backing from the institutional investors who will invest up to a further $100 million to establish one or more operational production sites from this pool of 12 possibilities over the next 12 months. However they have warned that any investment(s) must achieve a positive NPV over a 10 year period and must deliver payback within 4 years. YJ's pre-tax cost of capital is 15%.

Shah's discussions with the geologists, survey teams and also with Milo Purdeen and Jason Oldman who manage YJ's licence applications have revealed three potential fields which could be brought into production over the next 12 months. None of this information has, to date, been discussed outside YJ.

Option 1: EEE

This oil and gas field is in East Asia in a developing country which has suffered greatly from a long-term civil war and political unrest. The E&P industry is aware of the possibility of oil and gas reserves in this area but only a few companies have dug test wells so far due to the war and the ongoing political and economic uncertainty. Some companies which were present in the 1980s and 1990s have pulled out of this area following hijacks and violent attacks on oil vessels from pirates operating along the shoreline. The government of this country has just offered YJ an 8 year licence to start production at this field, which is expected to yield the following output:

Years	1-3	4-8
Oil – mmbbl	0.29	0.45
Gas – mmbble	0.46	0.61

The required initial investment in EEE would be $80 million and the net inflows from this field are expected to be 40% of the revenues.

Option 2: FFF

This oil and gas field is in the North Sea (UK waters), close to YJ's headquarters. The locality of the site and the well documented nature of the seabed in this area mean that YJ has incurred costs of only $5 million in surveying and exploring this site to date. As FFF is a larger field than the others that YJ is involved with, the required initial investment will be $180m. However the UK government will allow YJ a 50% share in a joint licence with another UK E&P company, a rival of YJ's called VZ, which means that YJ's investment will be $90m. YJ's share of this field's potential output over its 20 year lifespan will be as follows.

Years	1-5	6-20
Oil – mmbbl	0.39	0.61
Gas – mmbble	0.49	0.72

The net inflows from this field are expected to be 30% of the revenues.

Option 3: GGG

This oil and gas field is in one of the former republics of the Soviet Union in an area which has been extensively mined by local E&P companies already. There is some doubt over the potential yields of this field, however, as YJ's teams have not been given full access to the area. YJ has incurred $1.5 million in exploration and survey costs on this site and has applied for a 10 year licence. The government official has said this will certainly be granted to YJ upon receipt of a $5 million cash payment. The probable annual yields at this field are as follows:

	50% probability	30% probability	20% probability
Oil – mmbbl	0.61	0.39	0.36
Gas – mmbble	0.72	0.45	0.41

YJ's geologists believe that it will take a full year of pre-production work after the initial investment has been made before GGG begins to yield oil or gas. However the required initial investment in GGG, beyond the $5m licence payment, would only be $80 million, 50% of which would be incurred straightaway and 50% would be incurred one year later. The net inflows from this field are expected to be 30% of the revenues.

For the duration of all options described above, oil is expected to be sold at an average price of $110 per barrel and gas at an average price of $18 per barrel equivalent. Under government rules, none of the licences described above can be farmed out by YJ.

Valuation of YJ

Upon his appointment Ullan Shah promised the institutional investors an increase in YJ's production activity and a subsequent increase in profits and YJ's share price. The most significant pledge he offered shareholders was to achieve a share price for YJ of at least $29 by the next year end of 30 September 2014.

The share price of YJ is primarily driven by profitability and cashflow from its proven reserves combined with the market's confidence in the Board's ability to successfully bring further oil and gas fields into operation. It is expected that YJ could raise the finance required for the full amount of each investment by issuing shares at a 10% discount to today's share price.

The CFO has asked you to assess the potential impact of the three new potential fields described above upon the share price of YJ and to offer an assessment on which one will offer the best chance of achieving a share price of $29. YJ's share price today is $27.5 per share.

Oil leak at BBB

One of the engineers at BBB has reported the existence of a small underwater leak from one of the wells in the BBB oil and gas field. Crude oil from the wells is leaking into the ocean at a rate that currently falls within accepted legal tolerances set by the Asian country in question but it will cause some local pollution and these local legal standards are lax by international standards.

Adebe Ayrinde has been notified and has responded by asking for an update if the leak reaches the legal threshold at which YJ will become liable for penalties.

Commercial diving contractor

One of the most dangerous aspects of oil and gas exploration and production is the need for commercial "saturation" divers to work underwater for long periods at a time. Divers who are submersed beneath any significant depth for a period of time are at risk of decompression sickness – or "the bends" – when they rise to the surface and decompress. Saturation diving involves keeping the divers compressed at the surface, at underwater pressures, to reduce the risk of decompression, which can lead to death or severe injury. This technique also enables divers to work underwater for longer periods.

YJ has subcontracted its commercial diving requirements to RWD, a highly specialised UK based operator which is owned and managed by its founder Robin Winstanley, one of the original pioneers of saturation diving for commercial operations. Robin Winstanley is a world-renowned commercial diver and an expert in deep water and shallow water diving techniques. He and his team have an outstanding record for safety, efficiency, speed and the quality of the work performed. Many E&P companies in the UK and abroad would like to use the company because of the reputation and expertise of Robin Winstanley. However RWD is a deliberately small organisation focused on building client relationships and quality of service, and only provides its services to a small number of E&P companies worldwide, of which YJ was one.

Because much of the work performed by commercial divers is performed many miles offshore, it is usually more economical for E&P companies to put outsourced commercial diving contractors on retainer – whereby they are paid full rates for the entire duration of the drilling process even though they may not be required on every day or even for many days at a time. Therefore most E&P companies have retainer contracts with diving contractors which can be from 6 months to over 3 years in duration.

In November 2013 YJ renewed its 3 year retainer contract with RWD as the Board believed that the RWD's involvement in YJ's activities increased the company's profile and may even be a factor in YJ securing licences from governments in the future.

Last month Robin Winstanley was injured in a surface-based accident, unrelated to the work RWD was performing, at YJ's AAA site off the coast of Africa. He will be unable to dive commercially ever again and will be absent from RWD for at least one year. Adebe Ayrinde was furious as it was Robin's personal involvement which encouraged him to renew the contract, although the contract itself does not stipulate who will perform the work for YJ on behalf of RWD. Adebe Ayrinde immediately cancelled the contract with RWD and is about to appoint another commercial diving operator on a one year retainer at a cost of $7 million.

RWD has now filed a legal challenge against N for breach of contract.

Adebe Ayrinde has sought the advice of lawyers specialising in contract breaches and they have advised that if the case were to go to court and YJ was to lose the case, the cost including damages, could exceed $35 million. The chances of losing the case are assessed to be 50%. YJ currently has cash reserves of $14 million.

EEE licence application

The government of the East Asian country in which EEE is situated has recently offered a licence to YJ to drill for oil and gas over an 8 year period. YJ will either choose to drill this site themselves or write off the costs of exploration and the licence application to date.

Milo Purdeen has since announced to the Board that a member of his team has confessed to promising the government official responsible for awarding licences for EEE a significant cash payment for ensuring that YJ was offered the licence. This was completely unauthorised and the individual concerned acted alone in order to impress Milo Purdeen and the Board, claiming to be unaware of YJ's stance on such payments.

Although Milo Purdeen was furious, Ullan Shah was less concerned and explained to the Board that the EEE field could bring greater prosperity to this country and so by accepting the licence – irrespective of how it was obtained – YJ could argue it was acting in a socially responsible way. Jeremy Lion strongly disagreed and, supported by other members of the Board, argued that YJ's reputation was partially founded upon its ethical stance and that the government which awarded the CCC licence to YJ had emphasised this when it awarded the contract.

The Board would like you to assess the commercial implications for YJ of offering payments to government officials in order to win licences and to make appropriate recommendations. You have also been asked to comment separately on the ethical aspects of this practice.

End of Unseen Material

Mock Exam 2

YJ – Unseen material provided for mock exam 2

Additional (Unseen) information relating to the case is given on the following pages.

Read all of the additional material before you answer the question

---

ANSWER THE FOLLOWING QUESTIONS

The Finance Director of YJ has asked you, the management accountant, to provide advice and recommendations on the issues facing YJ.

Question 1 part (a)

Prepare a report that prioritises, analyses and evaluates the issues facing YJ and makes appropriate recommendations.

(Total marks for question 1a = 90 Marks)

Question 1 part (b)

As an appendix to the main report, prepare an email to Orit Mynde which summarises the results of the financial statements you have prepared together with your conclusions and recommendations.

(Total marks for question 1b = 10 Marks)

Note: Marks for calculations, relevant to Question 1 part (b), are awarded within the Assessment Criterion of Application included in Question 1 part (a).

Your script will be marked against the T4 Part b Case Study Assessment Criteria shown on the next page

Case Study Assessment Criteria

Analysis of Issues	25
Technical	5
Application	15
Diversity	5

Strategic Choices	35
Focus	5
Prioritisation	5
Judgement	20
Ethics	5
Recommendations	40
Logic	30
Integration	5
Ethics	5

ZZZ

When Ullan Shah was appointed as the new CEO he informed colleagues on the Board that he wanted to bring new oil and gas fields into operation at a much faster rate than had been achieved to date. In early December 2013, soon after joining YJ, Shah reviewed the 12 potential oil fields which were being surveyed by YJ's geological team and focused on one particular field off the east coast of Africa. This field is called ZZZ and YJ have not yet applied for a licence to produce oil and/or gas from this site.

ZZZ had first been surveyed by YJ at a cost of $4 million in June and July of 2011 and then a second survey had taken place in October and November of 2013 at a cost of $2.5 million and its results were discussed at a board meeting soon after Ullan Shah took over. At the board meeting, a proposal was put forward to discontinue investment in this field, as the results were not encouraging, and write off the costs to profit and loss in the same way that the 2011 costs had been written off. However Ullan Shah informed the Board that he disagreed with this proposal, because surveys which his previous company had performed in the same area some years ago had identified the possibility of significant reserves in deep water areas.

As a result, and against the advice of Milo Purdeen, he instructed subcontractors to drill the exploration wells in the deep water areas of this field which meant that further exploratory drilling took place at ZZZ around the end of 2013, at an additional cost of $15.5 million. All sums due have been paid to contractors in line with the 30 day terms agreed with YJ.

The results of this latest exploration revealed the presence of significant oil and gas reserves in a deep water area which could be expected to generate similar yields to YJ's AAA field once it is in the production phase. However YJ has never undertaken deep water drilling before and Adebe Ayrinde's research shows that it would be between 50% and 75% more costly to establish a deep water well in this area than a typical shallow water well elsewhere. These costs of production would be in addition to the exploratory costs already incurred. Ullan Shah is very keen to press ahead with this as he believes the share price will increase at the news of a new field coming into production. He also believes that YJ's strategic position will be strengthened if it can establish a deep water field to complement its existing shallow water fields as deep water fields can often yield output for longer periods.

Adebe Ayrinde and Milo Purdeen are against this idea, however. They believe the technological expertise required for deep water drilling and the inherent dangers involved make this a project which is beyond the risk appetite of YJ and its shareholders. Orit Mynde has also expressed his view that YJ should abandon its interests in ZZZ although this would mean writing off any sums incurred this year to the Profit or Loss Statement. Jeremy Lion has suggested that YJ recoup its investment in ZZZ by selling the results of its exploration to a larger E&P company or by obtaining a licence to drill the deep water area from the local government and then farming out the licence itself to a larger company with the necessary expertise. It is believed that the market value of the survey results already in YJ's possession would be approximately $7 million. Alternatively it is estimated that the costs of obtaining a licence would be $5 million and the potential net present value of farming out the licence to a larger company would be $30 million.

Jeremy Lion has made it clear that raising further equity finance during this accounting year is not acceptable to shareholders who are expecting a dividend within 12 months. Therefore any further investments made this year must be financed through operating cashflows and debt finance.

Orit Mynde has asked you for an assessment of these alternatives together with a recommendation supported by relevant financial analysis which he can present to the Board at next Monday's Board meeting.

Forecasts for the year end

Orit Mynde is under pressure from YJ's bank to produce full forecast financial statements to 30 September 2014, comprising a Profit or Loss Statement, Statement of Financial Position and a Statement of Cashflows. This is something which is routinely done at this time of year to comply with the bank's loan covenant which states that YJ's gearing level must not rise above 70% and that YJ's current ratio must exceed 1:1. If either of these conditions is breached then an immediate review of YJ's borrowings will take place and the institutional investors will be notified by the bank of its concerns. If the bank so chooses it can then invoke a guarantee clause in the loan covenants which prohibits YJ from paying dividends for two years after the year-end of the year in which the covenant is breached.

As Orit Mynde's assistant, you are responsible for providing him with the draft forecast financial statements referred to above together with your assessment of the results and appropriate recommendations.

You have established the following:

- The prices of oil and gas this year will be in line with the previous year

- Output from AAA and BBB will be the same as in the previous year

- CCC will increase its output of oil by 20% over 2012/13 but there will be no increase in its gas output in the period

- Gross margin will reduce to 41% as a result of cost increases in YJ's supply chain

- Distribution costs will increase by 60% as a result of increased activity from CCC

- Administrative expenses will increase by a rate of 10% of the increase in revenue

- There will be no change in finance costs, but no finance income

- New non-current assets capitalised in the year amount to $54 million in value and the annual depreciation charge will be $26 million

- Inventories will increase by 12%

- Trade receivables will be the same percentage of revenue as in the previous year

- Trade payables will increase by the same value as trade receivables

The above information does NOT take into account the impact of any decision in relation to ZZZ, nor any costs or revenues from the current accounting year in relation to ZZZ. Orit Mynde would like you to prepare the forecast financial statements assuming that his advice in relation to ZZZ is followed.

Maintenance contractor

YJ outsources most of its support activities, including essential maintenance of plant and machinery equipment at the oil and gas fields. "Maintenance" in this context includes necessary statutory testing of hazardous equipment, testing which is legally required by most international governments, including those governments which own the AAA, BBB and CCC oil and gas fields. If drilling takes place without this testing being up to date, then further drilling can be prohibited and very large fines can be imposed. In addition there is the increased health and safety risk of death or injury associated with the use of hazardous equipment which has not been fully serviced and tested. In commissioning the services of a maintenance contractor of this type, clients typically look for:

Factor	Meaning
Industry experience	Knowledge of the various contingent variables experienced at different oil and gas fields in different geographical areas, obtained over a period of time.
Global diversity	It is important for clients to receive a consistent and reliable service in this area across all their oil and gas fields.
Response time	Time taken between a request being made and a visit from a maintenance engineer being made.
Contract period	Duration of the contract and how long each party is locked into an agreement
Software compatibility	Some maintenance contractors supply automated software tool suites which enable clients to monitor safety indicators from within their own software systems – reducing exposure to risk, time and cost
Cost	The annual price of the service offered for each year of the contract

Some larger E&P oil and gas companies have vertically integrated their own maintenance divisions into their business, in some cases by purchasing standalone companies which provide this kind of service.

GTo is YJ's sole contractor for this kind of testing at all its oil and gas fields. GTo were first appointed in 2008 under a 3 year contract which was subsequently renewed in 2011 for a further 3 years. This company has offered excellent, prompt service to YJ throughout these years and, as well as ensuring that all the equipment's testing certificates are up to date, has frequently offered additional advice on equipment configurations and purchasing alternatives which has added value to YJ's operations.

This contract is due for renewal in 2 months. Last week YJ's customer account manager at GTo informed Adebe Ayrinde that the company is happy to renew the contract for a 3 further years with a 15% non-negotiable price increase applied. The annual cost of the existing contract, which covers all of YJ's global operations, is $22 million.

The Board was shocked and angry and is keen to explore alternative procurement strategies. Three potential alternative contractors have been identified and you have been asked for a preliminary assessment of each together with your recommendation. Information related to GTo has been included here for the purposes of comparison:

Supplier Name:	GTo	CK	QT	BT
Annual contract price	$22 million	$10 million	$15 million	$25 million
Areas covered	Global	• USA • Middle East • Africa • Canada • Russia • Asia	Global	• UK • Middle East • Africa • Russia • Asia
Company founded	1972	2009	1990	1981
Response time	2 days	7 days	6 days	1 day
Full software compatibility	Yes	No	Yes	Yes
Contract period	3 years	5 years	5 years	1 year
Market capitalisation	$100 million	$15 million	$40 million	$10 million

CK have offered Adebe Ayrinde a new car as a gift if he chooses to appoint CK as the contractor. Adebe explained this to the Board and Ullan Shah stated that this was commonplace in the oil and gas industry, especially from companies in certain parts of the world where CK are based. As there is no cost to shareholders because CK are the cheapest of all potential suppliers, Ullan has said there is no need to disclose this offer to shareholders.

CCC

This oil and gas field is off the coast of a South East Asian country called Country D. Milo Purdeen and Jason Oldman spent over a year trying to obtain this licence and became closely connected to the individual officials from within D's government responsible for the decision, attending many public functions together and even attending the wedding of a minister's daughter in full public view of the media. The government of D awarded a 10 year licence to YJ in 2012 to produce oil and gas from CCC in a 50:50 PSA with a royalty tax of 15% of revenues.

It has recently come to light in the world's media that citizens of D are being badly mistreated by the country's government and that there are serious concerns over human rights. There have been accusations of centralised racketeering by government officials, election rigging and coercion at voting stations whereby individuals have been threatened and even beaten into re-electing the government.

Lee Wang has suggested to the Board that YJ's continued presence in D is completely incompatible with its stated ethical stance and its CSR policies outlined on page 10 of the Preseen, as a collaborative working relationship with an unethical government makes YJ automatically unethical.

IT systems

YJ uses fully integrated IT systems which it initially installed in 2005 and which it has upgraded as and when needed. YJ pays annual software licence fees to the various supplying software companies and the systems are used by the whole of YJ. This system is critical to the day to day management of YJ's oil and gas fields and GTo's maintenance system is fully compliant with it. Further information on YJ's IT systems can be found on page 9 of the Preseen. Responsibility for IT lies with Orit Mynde's small finance department. All of YJ's 197 employees and many of the authorised subcontractors at the various fields across Asia and Africa use the system on a daily basis.

Under remote instruction from one of the IT systems' suppliers, EAG, the finance department in YJ installed a recently released upgraded software for the multi-currency nominal ledger last weekend, after all users had been informed that the system would be unavailable for the weekend. Back-ups of all systems' data were taken at the close of business last Friday. The upgraded version was then tested over the weekend and the finance department in YJ issued an email to all users on Monday morning of this week, informing them that the upgraded system was operational again. The finance department reminded all users about the new features of the upgraded multi-currency nominal ledger system and asked for any queries to be directed to Orit Mynde.

By the end of Tuesday of this week, 2 days after the upgrade was installed, Orit Mynde had received over 80 emails from YJ employees and contractors. He was totally overwhelmed by the volume of emails with queries and problems raised by users throughout YJ. He has chased, by phone and by email, his contact person at the software company, EAG, which has now admitted that it has other customers who are also experiencing some problems with the new software release.

Ullan Shah has asked Orit Mynde to check the integrity of the data contained in the IT systems of YJ and to investigate what data has been corrupted, as some employees and contractors have stated that oil and gas quantities and flow through rates have changed which makes it very difficult to know what reserves YJ is using and at what rate. Orit Mynde has also asked you to propose what actions should be taken now.

End of Unseen Material

SOLUTION
AND MARKING GRID

The solution that follows is a comprehensive answer showing the range of points and calculations you could undertake. As the marking grid shows, in the exam you would not need to make all the points in order to be awarded high marks.

ANSWER TO QUESTION 1A

REPORT

To: Chief Financial Officer

From: Management Accountant

Date: 2014

Contents

(1)   Introduction

(2)   Terms of reference

(3)   Identification and prioritisation of issues

(4)   Approaches to resolving the main issues

(5)   Ethical considerations

(6)   Recommendations

(7)   Conclusion

Appendices

(1)   SWOT analysis

(2)   CFROI

(3)   Email to FD

1 INTRODUCTION

YJ is a small E&P listed company. It is part of a massive global industry that depends on the extraction of finite resources at a cost that is lower than the resale value at prices determined by the market. Success for companies like YJ is determined by developing distinctive competences, for example an ability to focus on a geographic area like Salamander Energy (Asia), or on an unusual technology such as hydraulic fracking in the case of Cuadrilla Resources Limited. At the moment YJ appears to lack a specialism in either direction and as such risks being 'stuck in the middle' per Porter's generic strategy classification.

2 TERMS OF REFERENCE

This report identifies and evaluates the issues facing YJ and offers appropriate recommendations.

3 IDENTIFICATION AND PRIORITISATION OF ISSUES

The issues below have been prioritised based on the potential impact each could have combined with their urgency. A full SWOT analysis is presented in Appendix 1.

3.1– New Oil and Gas Fields

YJ has the opportunity to assess three new sites where it can potentially operate. This is a matter of high importance given the promise Ullan Shah made to investors of bringing more fields to production at a faster rate. The success of this is likely to determine the amount of future investment YJ receives, which means this issue must be explored as a matter of urgency. It is therefore ranked first in this report.

3.2 – Valuation of YJ

Given the importance of the above issue, it is also hugely important that YJ considers the individual impact on the share price for each of these potential ventures. The share price of YJ is vital given the high amount of investment it depends upon from investors. As no dividends have yet been paid to the investors of YJ, maintaining shareholder confidence that YJ is capable of delivering an acceptable share price is vital to ensure the company has the necessary financial resources to develop its business. It is therefore ranked second, behind the decision which will determine the valuation the market places on the shares

3.3 – Commercial diving contractor

This issue is urgent given that there is an imminent legal battle about to occur over the supposed breach of contract with RWD. There is a good chance that YJ will be liable for a bill of $35m and huge reputational damage, so it is very important to assess what options are available to mitigate this risk. However this issue is not fundamental to the long-term future of YJ and so is ranked behind the first two issues in this report.

3.4 – EEE licence application

YJ has recently won a contract for a site in Asia, which appears to have been swayed by a cash payment to an important representative from the government there. This issue needs to be resolved as it compromises the ethical stance that YJ takes and goes against the strong brand built up over many years.

This issue is less urgent as the above points because no payment has been made, and because shareholders who prioritise ethical issues are unlikely to be investing in the E&P sector. It is therefore ranked fourth in this report.

3.5 Other issues facing YJ

Other issues, such as the minor oil spill, have not been prioritised and ethical issues will be discussed in Section 5.

4 APPROACHES TO RESOLVING THE MAIN ISSUES

4.1– New Oil and Gas Fields

Impact

Ullan Shah has made a recent promise to investors that he will ensure that more sites are brought into production at a faster rate. There are three options available to YJ to consider in order to make this a reality and to repay the faith shown by investors, who have agreed to finance a further $100m. YJ needs to be careful, however, as although there is pressure to deliver these projects sooner, they must make both commercial and financial sense, otherwise they will destroy shareholder value. Financial analysis of each of the options can be found in appendix 2.

EEE

Benefits

EEE is located within Asia, an area that YJ currently carries out operations. If the area of Asia is located within YJ's current operational area then this move could provide a range of benefits associated with this type of strategic growth (Ansoff – market penetration). For example, supplier relationships will have been built up already, and local cultures and regulations should be well understood. Local contacts can also make it easier to secure contracts to sell natural gas – these are often made with local companies due to the problem of transporting natural gas. These benefits may make investment in this area smoother i.e. lower risk. Companies like Salamander Energy make a clear commitment to focussing on a narrow range of geographical areas for this reason.

Another benefit of investing here is that there has been little or no oil and gas production in the past, which increases the likelihood that there are large amounts of reserves present.

As can be seen in appendix 2, this option has the potential to yield a positive NPV of approximately $10 million and a payback period of 4.3 years. This is the highest NPV (over 10 years) and the lowest payback period of the options available (except for GGG under the most optimistic scenario). YJ's market capitalisation is currently $275 million (10m shares x $27.5) so this project would have the potential to raise market capitalisation by nearly 4%. There are, however, a number of risks inherent within this option that are explained below.

Drawbacks

This country has suffered greatly from long term civil war and political unrest. This presents a huge risk to YJ if it is to begin operations here if this were to continue as staff and operations may be at risk. The risk to staff and assets of operating in risky areas was visibly demonstrated by the massacre of a number of staff at an oilfield operated by BP in Algeria in 2013, This has historically resulted in it being very tough to do business in this area due to the political unrest and must be considered when looking at this option. It could be argued that this would justify a higher cost of capital to be used in the appraisal of this project.

Another risk with this option is that piracy has been an issue in recent years, which has resulted in companies not investing in oil and gas production. The threat of piracy represents a risk of expensive stock being stolen and presents safety risks to staff . In November 2013 near Malaysia an oil tanker was hijacked and all its contents were stolen. This was the second attack within four weeks, which highlights the problems in this area.

Another disadvantage of EEE is that it does not provide mitigation for geographical risk. YJ already has a lot of exposure to Asian areas, so it could be argued that a diversification of its portfolio could benefit shareholders by reducing risk. If a natural disaster were to occur, such as the Tsunami in 2004, this could hit YJ's operations drastically.

Finally the reference to digging test wells implies that this is on-shore and therefore is taking YJ into a type of drilling that it has no experience of, this adds to the risk of the project.

FFF

Benefits

FFF is based off the coast of the UK so is both local to YJ and provides diversity to its portfolio. This helps to spread risks in a manageable way given that YJ has considerable experience in off-shore drilling.

YJ will have to work with a competitor in this project. Although this may not be an ideal situation, YJ has the option to improve its operations on other projects if it learns how a key competitor operates.

Drawbacks

Co-operating with a competitor reduces the amount of control that YJ has, which may be difficult at first as YJ hasn't previously had to work with a competitor.

A joint venture of this type carries a number of risks:

- Slow decision making (especially with a 50:50 split)

- Operational disagreements (do the firms have a similar approach to environmental management, Health & Safety etc)

- Financial instability (e.g. if VZ has difficulty in raising its share of the investment)

Appendix 2 shows that this project produces an NPV of +$2.0m over 10 years and a payback period of 5.5 years. Although neither of these this is as attractive as the EEE investment, it is important to bear in mind that the licence is actually for 20 years and taking this into account the NPV rises to $31.83m. YJ's market capitalisation is currently $275 million (10m shares x $27.5) so this project would have the potential to raise market capitalisation by between 11% and 12%. The 20 year time horizon seems more appropriate especially because it is an established production area such as the North Sea, which carries less political risk (although there is always the risk of windfall taxes being imposed). However, the dilemma is that the shareholders appear to want to impose a 10 year time horizon for the NPV and a 4 year payback period.

GGG

Benefits

GGG is set in an area that is renowned for being rich with oil. This could mean that there is still a lot of oil for YJ to drill for, with plenty of expertise available in order to help YJ achieve this. This project will diversify YJ's operation which reduces the risks suggested above.

This project produces an NPV of +$0.8m under an expected value approach (see Appendix 2) and a payback of 4.4 years. However, this is subject to considerable uncertainty and the NPV carries a 50% chance of being negative, with a payback period in excess of 5 years. GGG would also require smaller set up costs, which could be very beneficial given the potential litigation issue (discussed in 4.3).

Drawbacks

YJ has struggled to gain full access to the land to conclude how much oil and gas is available to produce. This is reflected in the EV figures provided. Although there is a 50% chance of strong returns there is also a 50% chance that this site will be loss-making for YJ, which provides a risk to shareholder value and to Ullan Shah's commitment to increasing the share price.

As for EEE, this is an on-shore operation and therefore is taking YJ into a type of drilling that it has no experience of. This type of strategic move (Ansoff product development) adds to the risk of the project.

Another concern is that a government official has confirmed a payoff of $5m will secure the licence. This appears to go against YJ's ethics and causes potential brand risks should this be pursued. The risk of bribery potentially exposes YJ's Board to heavy fines and prison terms under the provisions of the Bribery Act (see section 4.4).

4.2 – Valuation of YJ

Impact

YJ's share price is a very important issue at present given that there is only 6 months before the price needs to increase. No dividends have been paid to investors and they have promised up to a further $100m recently in order to fund new projects. Investors may accept the lack of dividend if they see the value of their shares increase steadily, so ensuring the correct option is chosen in order to enhance shareholder value the most is pivotal to the successful future of YJ. This is an especially important issue because off the recent loss of Oliver Penn who until recently has been a key stakeholder (Mendelow's matrix) at YJ. So shareholder trust will need to be carefully managed.

In order to evaluate the future share price the three proposals in 4.1 need to be assessed.

EEE

As seen in appendix 3, the EEE project requires an extra 3.23m of shares to be issued. Even on the optimistic NPV which has been calculated at a cost of capital of 15% (as discussed in 4.1 there is an argument that the cost of capital should be higher for this project), the revised market price will be only marginally above the existing share price and will be well short of the required target.

FFF

As seen in appendix 3, the FFF project requires an extra 3.64m of shares to be issued. Assuming that the AIM is efficient to translate the NPV forecast into a higher share price there is the potential for the share price to rise significantly. If the market accept the full 20 year life of then project, and there does not appear any reason that it would not, then the share price should rise towards $29 and may even breach that level. However much will depend on the market price of oil and gas up to the end of September 2014.

GGG

Appendix 3 shows that under any scenario the GGG project is unlikely to achieve the promised target. As for EEE, this option would be high-risk for YJ, and as shareholders appear to be discounting for risk, this investment is very unlikely to boost the share price above $29. However, if the price of oil and gas increase then this venture will show more attractive returns.

4.3 – Commercial diving contractor

Impact

The loss of this contract is a huge disappointment for YJ given the excellent reputation of RWD. RWD is now filing for legal action, which presents huge financial and reputational risk for YJ. Company lawyers believe there is a 50% chance that $35m will need to be paid out which would put the business under strain. This would either have to be funded by expensive overdrafts or by investor funding and is highly likely to destroy shareholder value. The options below must be considered to mitigate this risk.

Option 1 – Settle out of court

As legal proceedings are barely underway there is an option to settle this dispute out of court now. A legal battle may be expensive for both sides. Given the loss of such an influential person, RWD may want to focus its attention on securing its own future. YJ could approach RWD with an offer to pay up for the first year of the contract, which is likely to cost in the region of $7m. YJ is able to afford this and it will mitigate any reputational risk that could result from a legal battle. However this is still a large payment, which could be avoided altogether in other options.

Option 2 – Agree to go to court

There is a 50% chance that YJ will be liable to pay nothing to RWD. YJ could take this chance agree to go to court and not have any expense to pay, potentially protecting its reputation if the issue is decided in its favour. This is a huge risk for YJ to take, however, and may not be approved by the board.

Option 3 – Countersue

If YJ believes that RWD has breached its side of the contract then YJ could countersue given the impact this has had on YJ's operations. Proposing to countersue could make this problem disappear completely or may provide cash for YJ, but if this is unsuccessful it may burden the company with more financial pressure.

4.4 – EEE licence application

Impact

YJ's CSR policy and ethical stance are integral to the future of the company. It takes a long time to build an ethical reputation. YJ's reputation has persuaded governments to grant it contracts and gained it respect from other stakeholders. Making a cash payment to ensure it is granted a licence is contrary to YJ's previous ethical stance and could have large commercial implications. It could for example jeopardise the future of the CCC project, which YJ was awarded because of its ethical reputation. **Option 1 – reject the licence**

YJ could choose to reject the licence now this information has come to light and refuse to deal with a government that accepts this behaviour

Option 2 – take incentive away but still table the bid

If Ullan Shah deals with this correctly, then YJ could accept the licence without the need for a bribe if the Asian country wishes to attract investment.

Option 3 – proceed with the licence

YJ could make the payment and accept the licence. However, this could also alienate other governments that are concerned about business ethics and force YJ to deal with governments that are less scrupulous. YJ may

also be criminally liable under anti-bribery legislation for failing to take sufficient steps to prevent employees making corrupt payments. All of this is likely to damage value very significantly as shareholders seek to offload their shares because they are concerned about YJ's poor ethics and the big risks arising from its unethical behaviour.

5 ETHICAL ISSUES

5.1 – Cash payments to governments

Why is this an ethical issue

This is morally wrong as the cash payment means that YJ is seeking to obtain work in an unfair way, and is not allowing fair competition. By paying a bribe YJ would also be helping to support and perpetuate an unfair culture. YJ would not be operating with integrity or in a professional manner. In addition, this information would have to be hidden from shareholders.

Recommendation for this ethical issue

YJ should discipline the member of staff that promised this payment. The Chairman should emphasise to Ullan Shah the risks highlighted in 4.4.

The company's ethical guidance be reviewed to ensure that it makes it clear that this type of behaviour is not tolerated, to avoid future reoccurrences.

5.2 – Oil leakages

Why is this an ethical issue

YJ has an obligation to protect the local areas that it works within. Although the current oil spillage is not breaching the local legal limits, it is still adversely affecting animals and humans alike. All creatures have the right to live in a safe environment and YJ should do all it can to ensure this happens, this is especially the case if by international standards the environmental standards in this area are lax.

Recommendation for this ethical issue

Adebe Ayrinde should appoint a team to assess this leak and the cost of fixing it. This will protect the local area and will prevent a future problem if the leak were to worsen.

In future, environmental reports should benchmark YJ's performance against best practice international standards, not just local standards.

6 RECOMMENDATIONS

6.1– New oil and gas fields

Recommendation

This report recommends that YJ first ensures that all preliminary and test work is completed thoroughly and not rushed before looking to proceed with the FFF licence.

Justification

Using Johnson Scholes Whittington SAF model, this strategy can be justified in that it is:

Suitable

This option provides diversification to YJ's geographic portfolio, which will mitigate area specific risks in the future, as well as providing potential synergies from working with a competitor. This has the potential to improve other YJ operations which will improve shareholder value. Applying for this licence also avoids the large risks associated with investment in both EEE and GGG.

Acceptable

Although this option does not achieve the required payback period, it is a long term investment that is likely to yield good returns over a 20 year period.

Feasible

Backing should be forthcoming from shareholders and the project involves off-shire drilling, which is YJ's core competence. [tutorial note – the SAF framework presented here is more commonly used in section 4 of the report to evaluate potential strategic decisions]

Actions to be taken

1. Complete preliminary work to high standard and ensure no corners are cut when assessing quality of the project

2. A shareholder meeting should be held to take the shareholders through this new project. It must be explained that the project won't achieve the payback period target but does come extremely close to achieving it and does have the advantages highlighted above

3. Ullan Shah should talk to all concerned parties directly to inform them of the direction that YJ wishes to take, being careful not to close any doors in case future options arise

4. YJ should meet with the rival company to discuss operations to avoid any issues arising from two competitors working together. Given the need for quick decision making, and bearing in mind that this is YJ's local country so YJ will also have the benefit of some local contacts, YJ should propose expanding its share of the venture from the proposed 50% to 55% - which is still affordable given its $100m budget. This would make YJ the lead partner and therefore better able to control environmental and health & safety risks. YJ should keep a close eye on competitors' operations, identifying good working practices that could be adopted at other locations

6.2 Valuation of YJ

Recommendation

This report recommends that YJ proceeds with the FFF option, although it may not quite deliver the promise Ullan Shah has made.

Justification

It could be an issue that this project does not deliver on the promise Ullan Shah has made, but it is critical that investors are made aware that this is a 20 year project, and success in a new, low-risk, area is likely to have favourable impacts on the share price.

Actions to be taken

1. Share price to be discussed at the same meeting highlighted in 6.1

2. Ensure buy in from investors, explaining the future benefit over 20 years arising from this secure option and risk mitigation

3. Proceed to work on FFF

4. Consult with YJ's merchant bank to see if the discount offered on the rights issue could be reduced, since this discount will have a depressing impact on the share price.

6.3 Commercial diving contractor

Recommendation

This report recommends that YJ attempts to settle out of court, offering payment for the first year of the contract as compensation (option 1).

Justification

The company lawyers have strong concerns that YJ may be liable to pay $35m compensation to RWD. This sum of money would wipe out cash reserves and put financial pressure on investors. Legal cases like this could result in huge reputation damage which would destroy shareholder value. Taking the above into account YJ should offer to compensate RWD with $7m to reduce the risk faced and to protect brand image.

Actions to be taken

1. Contact RWD to discuss out of court settlement of $7m, making clear this is the only offer to be tabled

2. Assuming this is accepted, proceed with the new contract that has been opened, providing that it is suitable for the company.

3. It is also important that Ullan Shah talks to Adebe Ayrinde about this as he has acted rather hastily in cancelling the contract. Mr Ayrinde needs to be aware that company lawyers need to be consulted on any decision that may result in a legal battle, thus allowing the YJ board to make well-informed decisions.

4. Reprimand Adebe Ayrinde and inform him of what is expected of a Director of YJ

6.4 EEE licence application

Recommendation

This report recommends that the licence is rejected (6.1). Further to this, the staff member involved must be disciplined.

Justification

Proceeding with this deal would go against the strong ethical background of YJ so should be completely rejected. This will protect the brand image of YJ, the investors and the board of directors alike. Other than the fact that this is against the values of YJ and probably illegal, EEE is a huge risk investment anyway, so pulling out of the licence negotiations makes commercial sense all round. Ullan Shah needs to be more aware of the importance of YJ's ethical stance to avoid future conflicts, and the Board should consider firing the member of staff involved, given the seriousness of the behaviour, to reduce the likelihood of this reoccurring.

Actions to be taken

1. Inform government that YJ is pulling out of the licence negotiations

2. Chairman to emphasise to Ullan Shah ethical stance and importance of preserving this

3. Discipline staff member and let all other staff know that this behaviour is unacceptable

 # 7 CONCLUSION

This report has identified and evaluated the issues facing YJ and has offered appropriate recommendations to enable Ullan Shah's ambitious growth plans to be successfully implemented.

Appendix 1: SWOT analysis

Strengths	Weaknesses
• Plenty of growth options available • Drive of Ullan Shah to deliver projects • Backing of investors	• Loss of inspirational leader of company • Some leakage issues • Staff making cash promises to win bids
Opportunities	**Threats**
• 3 new oil fields on offer • New direction under new CEO • Entering into farm in farm out contracts • Synergies in FFF contract	• Huge litigation case • CSR / reputation risk with oil leaks and bribes

Appendix 2: Analysis of new oil & gas fields

EEE

		0	1 to 3	4 to 8
payments	total PV	-80		
prodn	oil		0.29	0.45
	gas		0.46	0.61
revenue	oil		31.9	49.5
	gas		8.28	10.98
			40.18	60.48
net inflows (40%)			16.072	24.192
	df 15%		2.283	2.204
	PV		36.692	53.319
	total PV	90.011544		
	NPV	10.011544		
	Payback	-7.592	cumulative cash flow after 4 years	
		4.314	payback period	

FFF

		0	1 to 5	6 to 10	6 to 20
payments	total PV	-90			
prodn	oil		0.39	0.61	0.61
	gas		0.49	0.72	0.72
revenue	oil		42.9	67.1	67.1
	gas		8.82	12.96	12.96
			51.72	80.06	80.06
net inflows (30%)			15.516	24.018	24.018
	df 15%		3.352	1.667	2.907
	PV		52.010	40.038	69.820
	total PV	92.047638			

Analysis over 10 yrs	NPV	2.047638	**Payback**	-12.420 cumulative cash flow after 5 years
Analysis over 20 yrs	NPV	31.830		5.517 payback period

GGG

		0	1	high 2 to 10	med 2 to 10	low 2 to 10	EV 2 to 10
payments	licence	-5.000					
	invest	-40.000	-40.000				
	PV	-45.000	-34.783				
	total PV	-79.783					
prodn	oil			0.61	0.39	0.36	0.494
	gas			0.72	0.45	0.41	0.577
revenue	oil			67.1	42.9	39.6	54.34
	gas			12.96	8.1	7.38	10.386
				80.06	51	46.98	64.726
net inflows (30%)				24.018	15.300	14.094	19.418
	df 15%			4.149	4.149	4.149	4.149
	PV			99.651	63.480	58.476	80.564
	NPV			19.868	-16.303	-21.307	0.782
	Payback period			3.539	5.556	6.031	4.377

Note: the exploration costs of $1.5m for GGG are a sunk cost and have no impact on the NPV. In the event that GGG is not pursued then this amount might have to be written off, this may have a (minor) impact on the share price but it is assumed that this would be outweighed by the positive sentiment created by the decision to pursue the FFF option

Appendix 3: Valuation

Impact on share price

	EEE	FFF 10 years	FFF 20 years	GGG best case	GGG average	GGG worst	GGG EV
Current value of YJ	275	275	275	275	275	275	275
Extra capital injected	80	90	90	79.8	79.8	79.8	79.8
NPV from Appendix 2	<u>10</u>	<u>2</u>	<u>31.8</u>	<u>19.9</u>	<u>-16.3</u>	<u>-21.3</u>	<u>0.8</u>
Revised value of YJ	365.0	367.0	396.8	374.7	338.5	333.5	355.6
new shares issues (investment / 24.75)	3.23	3.64	3.64	3.22	3.22	3.22	3.22
total shares	13.23	13.64	13.64	13.22	13.22	13.22	13.22
price	27.58	26.91	29.10	28.33	25.60	25.22	26.89

Appendix 4: Presentation

1b

Email

To: Orit Mynde

From: Management accountant

Subject: Three proposals

Orit,

Please see my summary of the three proposals below. I have included both financial and non-financial factors to help explain my recommendations further.

EEE

This project provides an NPV of $10m and would in theory increase the share price to $27.6 by the end of the year. These financial measures would both be acceptable to shareholders. There are however many non-financial elements to consider with this option. EEE is based in a territory that has seen civil war and major unrest in recent time, as well as piracy. This would provide YJ with huge risks that may reduce the financial benefits highlighted above if shareholders discount for them.

FFF

This project is based in the UK and offers an NPV of up to $31.8m with a share price of up to $29.10. Although these do not achieve the required payback levels, the licence will last for 20 years, double that of the timescales used in NPV calculations. This also provides us with the opportunity to diversify our portfolio geographically and mitigate risks that may occur in areas we operate in.

GGG

This option is situated in a former Soviet republic, providing a positive expected value NPV of $0.8m but with high levels of risk that could actually depress the share price. Another issue here is the restrictions in testing the site thoroughly, meaning our decision is not as well-informed as others, providing major risks.

Recommendation

It is my recommendation that we proceed with FFF due to the good safe returns on offer over a long period of time and the spread of geographic risk.

Marking Grid for Mock Unseen

Criteria	Issues to be discussed	Marks	Total marks available
Technical	SWOT/PEST/Ansoff/Porter's 5 forces/Porter's generic strategies/Mendelow/Suitability, Acceptability, Feasibility/ BCG/Balanced Scorecard/Life cycle analysis/Marketing knowledge 1 mark for EACH technique demonstrated.	1 each max 5	Max = 5
Application	SWOT – to get full 3 marks the script must include all the Top 4 issues	1–3	Max = 15
	Other Technical Knowledge applied to case material in a meaningful relevant way – on merit	1–2 Max 5 for application of theory	
	Calculations:		
	NPV & payback	1-7	
	Valuations of YJ	1-5	
	Total marks available (but max = 15)	17	
Diversity	Display of sound business awareness and relevant real life examples related to case	1 mark each example used on merit	Max = 5
Focus (only award if issue is in the main report)	**Major issues to be discussed:**		Max = 5
	New oil and gas fields	1	
	Valuation of YJ	1	
	Commercial diving contractor	1	
	EEE	1	
	Total marks available – award 5 marks for 4 issues (but max = 5)	5	
Prioritisation	5 marks if 4 issues are prioritised and the rationale for ranking is good AND the top 2 issues are ranked in the correct order	5	Max = 5
	3–4 marks if top 2 priorities are in top 3 but ranking rationale is weak	3–4	
	2 marks maximum (marginal fail) if EITHER of the top 2 issues are not in top 3 priorities, irrespective of quality of rationale for ranking of other priorities	Up to 2	

Criteria	Issues to be discussed	Marks	Total marks available
Judgement	4 key and 1 minor issue available for detailed analysis in this case: Marks on merit based on depth of analysis and commercially realistic comments		Max = 20
	New oil and gas fields – full understanding of the significance of the numbers important here but a balance of financial and non-financial appraisal is needed	1–7	
	Valuation – basic calculations but ensure candidates have appreciated the positive impact on share price of low risk ventures with longer term yields (ie UK)	1–6	
	Commercial diving contractor – imaginative, commercial options required here (common sense)	1–5	
	EEE – an appreciation of how ethical dilemmas can have a commercial impact is tested here	1–4	
	Total marks available (but max = 20)	22	
Logic	**Recommendations:** (Marks on merit. Max 1 mark if only an unjustified recommendation is given)		Max = 30 Q1 (a) – 20 Q1 (b) – 10
	New oil and gas fields – the UK option is the most sensible here	0–7	
	Valuation – pursue a strategy which although it won't deliver the payback period requirement should give longer term benefits at a lower risk, possibly achieving the share price target	0–6	
	Commercial diving contractor – settle out of court. Unlikely that the companies can work together now	0–5	
	EEE - reject	0–5	
	Total marks available (but max = 20)	23	

Criteria	Issues to be discussed	Marks	Total marks available
QUESTION 1b	1 mark for each valid point. Look for a valid conclusion and appropriate use of financial information.	10	
	Total marks available	10	
Integration	Judge script holistically and whether recommendations follow on logically from analysis of the issues and refers to data in appendices. How well written is the report: professional language?	1–2 if weak 3–5 if script is good	Max = 5
Ethics	Ethical issues in case include: • Cash payment to government • Oil leakages	Up to 5 for identification and discussion of issues Up to 5 for recommend-ations on how to address those issues	Max = 10
Total			100

SOLUTION
AND MARKING GRID

The solution that follows is a comprehensive answer showing the range of points and calculations you could undertake. As the marking grid shows, in the exam you would not need to make all the points in order to be awarded high marks.

ANSWER TO QUESTION 1A

REPORT

To: Chief Financial Officer

From: Management Accountant

Date: 2014

Contents

(1)   Introduction

(2)   Terms of reference

(3)   Identification and prioritisation of issues

(4)   Approaches to resolving the main issues

(5)   Ethical considerations

(6)   Recommendations

(7)   Conclusion

Appendices

(1)   SWOT analysis

(2)   Forecasts

(3)   Email to Orit Mynde

INTRODUCTION

YJ is a small E&P listed company. It is part of a massive global industry that depends on the extraction of finite resources at a cost that is lower than the resale value at prices determined by the market. Success for companies like YJ is determined by either an ability to focus on a geographic area like Salamander Energy (Asia), or on an unusual technology such as hydraulic fracking in the case of Cuadrilla Resources Limited. At the moment YJ appears to lack a specialism in either direction and as such risks being 'stuck in the middle' per Porter's generic strategy classification.

TERMS OF REFERENCE

This report identifies and evaluates the issues facing YJ and offers appropriate recommendations.

3 IDENTIFICATION AND PRIORITISATION OF ISSUES

The issues below have been prioritised based on the potential impact each could have combined with their urgency. A full SWOT analysis is presented in Appendix 1.

3.1 – IT update issues

YJ has recently installed a new IT system update which seems to be filled with errors. This has had a major impact on the way YJ operates and is causing a huge issue on stock volume management right now. Given the cost of extracting oil and gas it is imperative that this problem is rectified as soon as possible to mitigate financial risk.

3.2 – Updated forecasts

YJ needs to submit forecasts to the bank. The latest forecast shows that there is a cashflow issue for YJ, as well as a breach of part of the loan covenant. This could have a huge impact on YJ's ability to raise further capital and must be addressed urgently.

3.3 – New oil field ZZZ

YJ has the option to drill for oil and gas in a new location that has vast amounts of natural resources available. There are many options to consider here, given the lack of expertise in deep drilling and the pressure from Ullan Shah to accept this proposal. If the decision made is an incorrect one the result could be heavily damaging for YJ.

3.4 – GTo contract

GTo currently holds the contract with YJ to look after maintenance and servicing of machinery in order to comply with strict regulations. This contract is up for renewal and YJ is faced with a 15% rise in the cost of the contract, which is over $3m. There are other options available which will be discussed, given that a decision needs to be made within two months.

3.5 Other issues facing YJ

Other issues have not been prioritised and ethical issues will be discussed in Section 5.

4 APPROACHES TO RESOLVING THE MAIN ISSUES

4.1 – IT update issues

Impact

A recent update to the IT system has seen many issues arise. This could have damaging impacts on YJ given that the system is critical for the day to day management of the company's oil and gas fields. If YJ does not resolve this issue immediately it will be close to impossible to make correct decisions, as its employees and contractors will not know how much oil and gas is being extracted and how much is being stored in reserve. If YJ does not have this information it does not know how much it can sell and at what price.. A sector that has had serious IT issues of late is the banking sector. For example RBS's IT platform has fallen over, not allowing customers to make payments. Other than the functionality of the business struggling greatly,

reputation damage will be tough to contain. A further impact is that all of YJ's suppliers link into this system too. If GTo cannot operate correctly on sites then YJ's drills may not even be operating legally, which puts even more risk into operations.

Option 1 – Revert back to old version immediately

Orit Mynde fortunately backed up all information the previous Friday, so it is a viable option to remove the software update and revert back to the previous version. Although moving forward this is likely to work, it does not resolve stock issues that have occurred since the new update went active, so any missed information is unlikely to be recoverable.

Option 2 – Contact EAG to sort this matter, seeking compensation

Orit Mynde could contact EAG and instruct it to resolve this issue immediately. As a valued customer of EAG, YJ has an element of customer power here, which should encourage EAG to help out straight away. EAG is likely to be able to resolve this issue quickly, which is a strong benefit to YJ, but again this does not resolve the issues that have happened over the past two days. Orit should inform EAG that if this issue is not resolved within two days and compensation paid then they will look for a new IT solution.

Option 3 – Purchase new single system

There are likely to be many other IT solutions available. YJ could use this opportunity to upgrade its systems to more state of the art systems that are likely to be working straight away. Although this is likely to be beneficial moving forward, YJ currently is in a good position where all staff and suppliers know how to work the current systems, so this could be a very costly and time consuming solution. There may be problems over contracts with other existing suppliers.

Option 4 – Manual reconciliation of all stock

Ullan Shah could instruct Orit Mynde to conduct a manual reconciliation of all stock in order to provide the most accurate view of the business over the past two days. This would be hugely beneficial for decision making, and twinned with either option 1 or option 2 could resolve the issue for YJ. This is likely to be a complex piece of work that takes time, however, which could mean the issues get much worse before they get better.

4.2 – Updated forecasts

Impact

The CFO has asked for forecasts to be updated for reporting to the bank. These forecasts reveal a drastic reduction in cash resources over the next 9 months, which in turn results in the current ratio breaching the covenant. This would have major impacts on YJ as shareholders will be troubled by this information, as they will have no dividends for the next two years. This could well result in investors selling their shares which will reduce the share price of YJ, and make it much tougher to obtain capital investment in the future. Oil and gas production is a highly capital intensive industry, so loss of shareholder confidence is something that must be avoided at all costs. Olympus cameras reported a breach in its loan covenant in 2012 which resulted in parent company Oki Electric's share price falling by 33%, something that must be avoided here. Solutions are provided below in order to better manage the cash flow position so that no breach is reported.

Option 1 – Sell ZZZ survey for $7m

YJ currently has an important decision to make over whether to invest in ZZZ. There is an option to sell current findings for around $7m, which would boost the current ratio to around 1.12. This would alleviate the current risk, but ZZZ has the chance of being a highly lucrative drilling operation for YJ in future.

Option 2 – Cut costs by further outsourcing

Outsourcing is a model that YJ operates at the moment and is a quick way to reduce costs. YJ could look to outsource more of its operations to reduce this cost and improve the cash flow position. However, given that YJ already outsources a lot of operations, it may not have much more scope to outsource more without losing control of the business. In addition if YJ outsources too many of its operations it may lose sight of what its core competencies are.

Option 3 – Appoint CK or QT for maintenance contracts

CK & QT are offering a much cheaper deal than GTo and they would save either $12m or $7m compared with GTo's existing price. This will clearly provide a cash benefit and improves the current ratio. Although this would resolve the issue, these contracts are cheaper for a reason and the quality of service may suffer as a result, thus not making this a long term solution.

Option 4 – Call in debtors and renegotiate payment terms

If YJ renegotiates its payment terms then it will improve the cash flow position if accepted. Extending terms with suppliers is something that happens frequently in the market place but is generally a sign of weakness to investors and indicates a company that is having cash flow difficulties, which may have the same impact as breaching the covenant anyway.

Option 5 – Prepare shareholders for bad news

YJ could inform shareholders that the breach is likely to occur and that they should be prepared to forego dividends. This is likely to be unacceptable, so will not be considered in this report.

4.3 – New oil field ZZZ

Impact

YJ has the opportunity to drill for oil and gas at a site which has many natural reserves present. If successful this is likely to delight shareholders and boost income in YJ for many years to come. There are many constraints in force around YJ at the moment as discussed above, which must be considered when looking at potential options here. ZZZ requires deep extraction given the depth of the oil here, something which YJ is not familiar with. This does increase the risk profile of this solution.. Given the constraints and risks present here it is vital to consider the following options carefully.

Option 1 – Drill for oil

The research shows that there is substantial oil and gas at site ZZZ, thus making this project one with high potential. If YJ was to succeed here it would open up many further avenues for them to move into deep extraction locations globally, and will greatly enhance the reputation and share price.

There are many concerns with this option though, as cashflow is a huge constraint for YJ at present. Deep extraction is much more costly than shallow extraction, which puts further pressure on the cashflow forecast, and YJ would also be required to source the $5m funds to obtain the licence. This, twinned with the fact that deep extraction is not something that YJ has any experience of, puts huge risk into the project, and is likely to destroy shareholder value.

Option 2 – Sell current findings

Jeremy Lion has suggested that current findings can be sold and indications are that YJ will obtain around $7m for them. This would result in YJ losing $11m on this project in total, but recouping $7m is better than losing even more money. This sale will result in YJ not breaching the covenant, which will reduce any reputation risk and alleviate cashflow pressures in the short term.

One thing to consider here is that YJ may look weak to shareholders in selling this information. Shareholders want to see steady growth, and ignoring an option that could make $30m in net present value will raise questions on what direction the company is taking.

Option 3 – Accept licence and sell

YJ could pursue the licence and then farm out the licence to a larger firm for $30m. This appears to be a sensible solution as it reduces the risk YJ faces and will allow it to capitalise on a site that has huge natural reserves present. In the long term this is a positive solution, but YJ will still breach the covenant to the bank and provide huge short term risks.

4.4 – GTo contract

Impact

The GTo contract is one that is very important to YJ as this seamless relationship has allowed YJ to operate within legal requirements for many years. It is important that this work is completed accurately, punctually and to the highest standard for YJ to remain operational. An increase of 15% in the contract is a pure cost to the P&L, so other options need to be considered.

GTo

The relationship with GTo has worked well for many years. GTo offers a global service so allows YJ the freedom to set up fields at any site. With a short response time, compatibility with IT services and proven history in delivering this is a great fit with our company. The expense of contract must be considered, and the way that GTo has demanded a 'non-negotiable' price increase is not how to deal with a customer such as YJ that has been loyal for a long time.

CK

CK was only founded 5 years ago and does not have a large share of the market. Although it does not cover global areas it does cover our main areas at present for a more than 50% reduction on the cost GTo is proposing. Although cost is important, it would take CK 7 days to respond to any issue we have, which could halt the production of oil and drastically reduce profitability if a drill is not functioning. IT issues could also arise given the lack of compatibility.

QT

The QT contract offers global coverage, which would allow YJ to expand with no concerns, at a $7m reduction in cost to GTo. The longer contract period here could work in favour of YJ too given the low cost discussed. Full software compatibility is an advantage that QT has compared with CK. The lead time of 6 days is the main concern here, as the extra 4 days response compared to GTo could result in a huge reduction in production.

BT

BT has a response time of 1 day, which is the best on offer and should minimise stoppages. BT also covers YJ's operational areas at present and has full software compatibility. Concerns here are the expense of the contract and the short length of the deal, meaning prices may rise further next year.

 # 5 Ethical issues

5.1 – Offer of a car incentive to Adebe Ayrinde

Why is this an ethical issue

Although it does not appear to be clearly unethical to offer a car as an incentive in this position, YJ has at least a moral obligation to be honest and transparent with shareholders. This is required in order for shareholders to make an informed decision.

Recommendation for this ethical issue

YJ should disclose to shareholders that CK has offered a car incentive if YJ picks CJ as the supplier. Jeremy Lion needs to inform Ullan Shah that being open and honest is morally correct and should be a given when working for such an ethical company such as YJ. It may be most prudent in any case to decline the offer of the car..

5.2 – Issue in Country D

Why is this an ethical issue

YJ has had a strong relationship with the government in country D. Its oppressive behaviour is a dilemma for YJ. Bad treatment of citizens, election rigging and coercion are all clearly immoral, but it is not strictly unethical for YJ to continue operating there.

Recommendation for this ethical issue

YJ must end directors' close relationship with the government of country D in order to distance itself from the government's behaviour. YJ should continue to operate on project CCC as this is a very favourable one to the company, but caution must be taken with this issue. In particular YJ must be sure that its continued operations in D are compatible with what it says about the ethical standards it aims to maintain.

6 RECOMMENDATIONS

6.1– IT update issue

Recommendation

This report recommends that YJ calls in EAG to resolve this issue immediately, whilst performing a manual reconciliation at the same time. Further to this a dedicated Head of IT is required to alleviate this pressure from the CFO.

Justification

Given that this system is EAG's product it is likely to be able to correct this in the most efficient manner. The threat of cancelling this contract if the issue is not resolved is likely to be incentive enough for EAG to sort this issue out promptly. If YJ was to remove the software update and revert back to the previous version there is no telling yet whether this would indeed work, so to mitigate this risk as soon as possible positive action is required. It is important that Finance completes a manual reconciliation of all production so that it is aware of exactly what has been produced and sold. Orit Mynde should also employ a Head of IT that reports to him, as it is not feasible for a Director of YJ to receive this many emails on the matter.

Actions to be taken

1. Contact EAG immediately and inform it that YJ wants a solution to the problems associated with the update immediately, whether this be a correction or reverting back to the previous platform

2. Instruct Finance to begin reconciliation of all stock movement and production over the past week

3. Inform production teams to manually count their production until further notice until this issue is resolved

4. Employ Head of IT to be closer to these issues moving forward to mitigate future risk

6.2 Updated forecasts

Recommendation

This report recommends that YJ sells the current findings of ZZZ for $7m. In addition to this YJ should aim to renegotiate the GTo contract and reduce this cost.

Justification

If YJ sells the findings of ZZZ it is no longer in breach of the covenant which is the ultimate desired result. The fact that ZZZ provides a huge risk to YJ anyway supports this issue. Although selling this information makes sense from a short term financial position, it is hugely important that YJ walks the shareholders through this journey, as YJ will be letting an opportunity for increased future profits go. Although this may be a tough option to digest for some, the short term future of the company must be secured before foundations can be set for the future. YJ should also look to reduce the cost of the GTo contract to boost the cash flow position. A key issue from this will be for the CFO to talk through all aspects of YJ's financial position with Ullan Shah, as ultimately the $15m cost that he has insisted be incurred has put the company under huge financial strain.

Actions to be taken

1. CFO to inform Ullan Shah on recommendations and rationale

2. Ensure shareholders are aware of the decision and the justification for this

3. Sell the findings for the highest price possible whilst renegotiating the GTo deal

6.3 New oil field ZZZ

Recommendation

As suggested above, this report recommends that YJ seeks to sell the findings for at least $7m. If there are any significant changes to cashflow in the short term aside from this, then option 3 should be considered.

Justification

Although there is much oil and gas available to pump from site ZZZ, the inherent risks to a smaller E&P company such as YJ are too great for it to proceed with drilling at this site. YJ's core specialty is shallow drilling, so moving into deep drilling at a time where both cashflow and capital investment are low is a not a risk that should be taken. This result also should mean that YJ does not breach the covenants in September 2014. This report does note that if extra cashflow did arise not mentioned in this report then YJ should look to obtain the licence and farm out the contract to a larger company, as this would be hugely profitable in the future. This report acknowledges however the short term solution based upon this information is that the $7m receipt is pivotal for the company to continue without being pressurised by the bank and preserve shareholder value.

Actions to be taken

1. Sell findings at the earliest convenience

2. CFO to discuss rationale with Ullan Shah

3. Do not investigate any further deep drilling sites until cashflow improves

6.4 GTo contract

Recommendation

This report recommends that YJ seeks to renegotiate the deal, referring to the very competitive deal tabled by CK and the long relationship in place.

Justification

GTo is a perfect strategic fit for YJ in terms of geographic coverage and response time. They have worked together for a long time already. This relationship has never provided an issue in the past, and should not result in any loss of production due to legal issues with the drills being used, YJ needs to renegotiate the deal, however, as it needs to avoid being held to ransom by suppliers. GTo is likely to reduce the price increase if negotiated correctly as CK does provide a potential replacement given the $12m reduction in contract cost. Even if GTo refuses to budge, YJ should accept this contract given the seamless manner in which the operation currently works.

Actions to be taken

1. Contact GTo on reduction to contract offer threatening to move to CK

2. Proceed to deal with GTo

 # CONCLUSION

This report has identified and evaluated the issues facing YJ and has offered appropriate recommendations.

Appendix 1: SWOT analysis

Strengths	Weaknesses
• Relationship with supplier GTo • Passion of Ullan Shah	• Lack of investment available this year • Directing IT queries straight to the CFO • Lack of experience in deep extraction
Opportunities	**Threats**
• ZZZ contract • New maintenance contract • Moving into deep extraction	• Reputation being linked to unethical practice in country D • Update in IT system • Rising cost of maintenance • Cash flow risk and breach of covenant

Appendix 2: Forecasts

Income statement

[tutor note - this analysis assumes that the cost of sales is $124.4m – this is calculated as 59% of revenue (the question says that margin is 41% so costs are (1-0.41) 59% of revenue) plus $18m of exploration costs of (15.5m + 2.5m) spent in 2013/14. The assumption that the $18m is not-capitalised has been made because we are using the CFO's view that this is not an economically viable proposal so the costs need to be written off – we are told to adopt this view in the exam]

	Year ended 30-Sep-14 €m
Revenue	180.4
Cost of sales	124.4
Gross profit	56.0
Distribution costs	0.8
Administrative expenses	22.7
Operating profit	32.5
Finance expense	15.6
Profit before tax	16.9
Tax expense (24%)	4.0
Profit for the period	12.8

Statement of financial position and key ratios

	As at 30-Sep-14 €m	As at 30-Sep-13 €m
Non-current assets (net)	217.0	189.0
Current assets		
Inventory	28.0	25.0
Trade receivable	6.7	6.5
Cash and cash equivalents -	1.0	13.6
Total assets	250.7	234.1
Equity and liabilities		
Equity		
Share capital	10.0	10.0
Share premium	50.0	50.0
Retained earnings	14.5	1.7
Total equity	74.5	61.7
Non-current liabilities		
Long term loans	140.0	140.0
Current liabilities		
Liability for acquisition	-	-
Trade payables	32.1	31.9
Tax payables	4.0	0.5
Total current liabilities	36.1	32.4
Total equity and liabilities	250.7	234.1
Gearing	0.65	0.69
Current ratio	0.93	1.39

Statement of cashflows

	€m
Cash flows from operating activities	
Profit before taxation (after Finance costs (net))	16.9
Adjustments:	
Depreciation	26
Finance costs	15.6
	41.6
(Increase)/decrease in inventories	-3
(Increase)/decrease in trade receivables	-0.2
Increase/(decrease) in trade payables (excluding taxation)	0.2
	-3
Finance costs paid	-15.6
Tax paid	-0.5
Cash generated from operating activities	**39.4**
Cash flows from investing activities	
Purchase of non-current assets	-54
Cash flows from financing activities	
Dividends paid	
Net increase in cash and cash equivalents	**14.6**
Cash at start of the year	13.6
Cash at end of the year	**1.0**

Appendix 3: Email to Orit Mynde

Email

To: Orit Mynde

From: Management Accountant

Subject: Financial statement

Hi Orit,

After completing the recent view of the 2014 forecast there are some clear issues that have been highlighted.

The first thing to point out is that we are currently set to breach the covenant in September, as the current ratio is set to reduce to 0.93.

One of the reasons for this is the impact on the cash flow position, which is set to drop by $15m over the year to a negative position of $1.0m.

The gearing position improves and does not breach the covenant.

It is clear that we must review the cash flow position in order to reduce high overdraft costs and so that we do not breach the covenant.

Actions to improve cash flow

In order to improve cash flow I recommend that we seek to sell the investigative work done on site ZZZ.

This will generate a further $7m of cash for the company and result in a positive current ratio, meeting covenant requirements.

If more drastic action is required YJ should look to renegotiate the GTo contract, or even look at change this contract to CK to provide improved cash flow.

Many thanks

Management accountant

Marking Grid for Mock 2 Unseen

Criteria	Issues to be discussed	Marks	Total marks available
Technical	SWOT/PEST/Ansoff/Porter's 5 forces/Porter's generic strategies/Mendelow/Suitability, Acceptability, Feasibility/ BCG/Balanced Scorecard/Life cycle analysis/Marketing knowledge 1 mark for EACH technique demonstrated.	1 each max 5	Max = 5
Application	SWOT – to get full 3 marks the script must include all the Top 4 issues	1–3	Max = 15
	Other Technical Knowledge applied to case material in a meaningful relevant way – on merit	1–2 Max 5 for application of theory	
	Calculations:		
	P&L	1-3	
	SOFP	1-3	
	Cashflow	1-3	
	Gearing and current ratios	1-2	
	Total marks available (but max = 15)	16	
Diversity	Display of sound business awareness and relevant real life examples related to case	1 mark each example used on merit	Max = 5
Focus (only award if issue is in the main report)	**Major issues to be discussed:**		Max = 5
	IT issues	1	
	Updated forecasts	1	
	ZZZ oil field	1	
	GTo contract	1	
	If all issues discussed in full	1	
	Total marks available – award 5 marks for 4 issues (but max = 5)	5	
Prioritisation	5 marks if 4 issues are prioritised and the rationale for ranking is good AND the top 2 issues are ranked in the correct order	5	Max = 5
	3–4 marks if top 2 priorities are in top 3 but ranking rationale is weak	3–4	
	2 marks maximum (marginal fail) if EITHER of the top 2 issues are not in top 3 priorities, irrespective of quality of rationale for ranking of other priorities	Up to 2	

Criteria	Issues to be discussed	Marks	Total marks available
Judgement	4 key and 1 minor issue available for detailed analysis in this case: Marks on merit based on depth of analysis and commercially realistic comments		Max = 20
	IT issues – award up to 2 marks for each option discussed in full	1–7	
	Updated forecasts – Max 2 marks if no options to resolve the cash problems are discussed	1–7	
	New Oil Field – up to 2 marks per option discussed	1–6	
	GTo – need to discuss all 4 options as a minimum to score > 3mks	1–5	
	Total marks available (but max = 20)	25	
Logic	**Recommendations:** (Marks on merit. Max 1 mark if only an unjustified recommendation is given)		Max = 30 Q1 (a) – 20 Q1 (b) – 10
	IT issues – must recommend some immediate and positive action	0–7	
	Updated forecasts – marks are awarded ONLY for discussion on how to resolve credit crunch i.e farm-outs, sale of ZZZ etc	0–7	
	New Oil Field – ZERO marks if development is recommended without a realistic finance package i.e farm-out / bank loan etc. Cap marks at 2 if development is recommended.	0–6	
	GTo – cap marks at 2 if any provider but GTo is recommended	0–5	
	Total marks available (but max = 20)	25	

Criteria	Issues to be discussed	Marks	Total marks available
QUESTION 1b	1 mark for each valid bullet point.	10	
	Total marks available	10	
Integration	Judge script holistically and whether recommendations follow on logically from analysis of the issues and refers to data in appendices. How well written is the report: professional language?	1–2 if weak 3–5 if script is good	Max = 5
Ethics	Ethical issues in case include: • Offer of Car • Working in D	Up to 5 for identification and discussion of issues Up to 5 for recommend-ations on how to address those issues	Max = 10
Total			100

APPENDIX

MATHEMATICAL TABLES AND EXAM FORMULAE

Present value table

Present value of 1.00 unit of currency ie $(1+r)^{-n}$ where r = interest rate, n = number of periods until payment or receipt.

Periods	Interest rates (r)									
(n)	1%	2%	3%	4%	5%	6%	7%	8%	9%	10%
1	0.990	0.980	0.971	0.962	0.952	0.943	0.935	0.926	0.917	0.909
2	0.980	0.961	0.943	0.925	0.907	0.890	0.873	0.857	0.842	0.826
3	0.971	0.942	0.915	0.889	0.864	0.840	0.816	0.794	0.772	0.751
4	0.961	0.924	0.888	0.855	0.823	0.792	0.763	0.735	0.708	0.683
5	0.951	0.906	0.863	0.822	0.784	0.747	0.713	0.681	0.650	0.621
6	0.942	0.888	0.837	0.790	0.746	0705	0.666	0.630	0.596	0.564
7	0.933	0.871	0.813	0.760	0.711	0.665	0.623	0.583	0.547	0.513
8	0.923	0.853	0.789	0.731	0.677	0.627	0.582	0.540	0.502	0.467
9	0.914	0.837	0.766	0.703	0.645	0.592	0.544	0.500	0.460	0.424
10	0.905	0.820	0.744	0.676	0.614	0.558	0.508	0.463	0.422	0.386
11	0.896	0.804	0.722	0.650	0.585	0.527	0.475	0.429	0.388	0.350
12	0.887	0.788	0.701	0.625	0.557	0.497	0.444	0.397	0.356	0.319
13	0.879	0.773	0.681	0.601	0.530	0.469	0.415	0.368	0.326	0.290
14	0.870	0.758	0.661	0.577	0.505	0.442	0.388	0.340	0.299	0.263
15	0.861	0.743	0.642	0.555	0.481	0.417	0.362	0.315	0.275	0.239
16	0.853	0.728	0.623	0.534	0.458	0.394	0.339	0.292	0.252	0.218
17	0.844	0.714	0.605	0.513	0.436	0.371	0.317	0.270	0.231	0.198
18	0.836	0.700	0.587	0.494	0.416	0.350	0.296	0.250	0.212	0.180
19	0.828	0.686	0.570	0.475	0.396	0.331	0.277	0.232	0.194	0.164
20	0.820	0.673	0.554	0.456	0.377	0.312	0.258	0.215	0.178	0.149

Periods	Interest rates (r)									
(n)	11%	12%	13%	14%	15%	16%	17%	18%	19%	20%
1	0.901	0.893	0.885	0.877	0.870	0.862	0.855	0.847	0.840	0.833
2	0.812	0.797	0.783	0.769	0.756	0.743	0.731	0.718	0.706	0.694
3	0.731	0.712	0.693	0.675	0.658	0.641	0.624	0.609	0.593	0.579
4	0.659	0.636	0.613	0.592	0.572	0.552	0.534	0.516	0.499	0.482
5	0.593	0.567	0.543	0.519	0.497	0.476	0.456	0.437	0.419	0.402
6	0.535	0.507	0.480	0.456	0.432	0.410	0.390	0.370	0.352	0.335
7	0.482	0.452	0.425	0.400	0.376	0.354	0.333	0.314	0.296	0.279
8	0.434	0.404	0.376	0.351	0.327	0.305	0.285	0.266	0.249	0.233
9	0.391	0.361	0.333	0.308	0.284	0.263	0.243	0.225	0.209	0.194
10	0.352	0.322	0.295	0.270	0.247	0.227	0.208	0.191	0.176	0.162
11	0.317	0.287	0.261	0.237	0.215	0.195	0.178	0.162	0.148	0.135
12	0.286	0.257	0.231	0.208	0.187	0.168	0.152	0.137	0.124	0.112
13	0.258	0.229	0.204	0.182	0.163	0.145	0.130	0.116	0.104	0.093
14	0.232	0.205	0.181	0.160	0.141	0.125	0.111	0.099	0.088	0.078
15	0.209	0.183	0.160	0.140	0.123	0.108	0.095	0.084	0.079	0.065
16	0.188	0.163	0.141	0.123	0.107	0.093	0.081	0.071	0.062	0.054
17	0.170	0.146	0.125	0.108	0.093	0.080	0.069	0.060	0.052	0.045
18	0.153	0.130	0.111	0.095	0.081	0.069	0.059	0.051	0.044	0.038
19	0.138	0.116	0.098	0.083	0.070	0.060	0.051	0.043	0.037	0.031
20	0.124	0.104	0.087	0.073	0.061	0.051	0.043	0.037	0.031	0.026

Cumulative present value table

This table shows the present value of 1.00 unit of currency per annum, receivable or payable at the end of each year for n years $\dfrac{1-(1+r)^{-n}}{r}$.

Periods (n)	Interest rates (r)									
	1%	2%	3%	4%	5%	6%	7%	8%	9%	10%
1	0.990	0.980	0.971	0.962	0.952	0.943	0.935	0.926	0.917	0.909
2	1.970	1.942	1.913	1.886	1.859	1.833	1.808	1.783	1.759	1.736
3	2.941	2.884	2.829	2.775	2.723	2.673	2.624	2.577	2.531	2.487
4	3.902	3.808	3.717	3.630	3.546	3.465	3.387	3.312	3.240	3.170
5	4.853	4.713	4.580	4.452	4.329	4.212	4.100	3.993	3.890	3.791
6	5.795	5.601	5.417	5.242	5.076	4.917	4.767	4.623	4.486	4.355
7	6.728	6.472	6.230	6.002	5.786	5.582	5.389	5.206	5.033	4.868
8	7.652	7.325	7.020	6.733	6.463	6.210	5.971	5.747	5.535	5.335
9	8.566	8.162	7.786	7.435	7.108	6.802	6.515	6.247	5.995	5.759
10	9.471	8.983	8.530	8.111	7.722	7.360	7.024	6.710	6.418	6.145
11	10.368	9.787	9.253	8.760	8.306	7.887	7.499	7.139	6.805	6.495
12	11.255	10.575	9.954	9.385	8.863	8.384	7.943	7.536	7.161	6.814
13	12.134	11.348	10.635	9.986	9.394	8.853	8.358	7.904	7.487	7.103
14	13.004	12.106	11.296	10.563	9.899	9.295	8.745	8.244	7.786	7.367
15	13.865	12.849	11.938	11.118	10.380	9.712	9.108	8.559	8.061	7.606
16	14.718	13.578	12.561	11.652	10.838	10.106	9.447	8.851	8.313	7.824
17	15.562	14.292	13.166	12.166	11.274	10.477	9.763	9.122	8.544	8.022
18	16.398	14.992	13.754	12.659	11.690	10.828	10.059	9.372	8.756	8.201
19	17.226	15.679	14.324	13.134	12.085	11.158	10.336	9.604	8.950	8.365
20	18.046	16.351	14.878	13.590	12.462	11.470	10.594	9.818	9.129	8.514

Periods (n)	Interest rates (r)									
	11%	12%	13%	14%	15%	16%	17%	18%	19%	20%
1	0.901	0.893	0.885	0.877	0.870	0.862	0.855	0.847	0.840	0.833
2	1.713	1.690	1.668	1.647	1.626	1.605	1.585	1.566	1.547	1.528
3	2.444	2.402	2.361	2.322	2.283	2.246	2.210	2.174	2.140	2.106
4	3.102	3.037	2.974	2.914	2.855	2.798	2.743	2.690	2.639	2.589
5	3.696	3.605	3.517	3.433	3.352	3.274	3.199	3.127	3.058	2.991
6	4.231	4.111	3.998	3.889	3.784	3.685	3.589	3.498	3.410	3.326
7	4.712	4.564	4.423	4.288	4.160	4.039	3.922	3.812	3.706	3.605
8	5.146	4.968	4.799	4.639	4.487	4.344	4.207	4.078	3.954	3.837
9	5.537	5.328	5.132	4.946	4.772	4.607	4.451	4.303	4.163	4.031
10	5.889	5.650	5.426	5.216	5.019	4.833	4.659	4.494	4.339	4.192
11	6.207	5.938	5.687	5.453	5.234	5.029	4.836	4.656	4.486	4.327
12	6.492	6.194	5.918	5.660	5.421	5.197	4.988	7.793	4.611	4.439
13	6.750	6.424	6.122	5.842	5.583	5.342	5.118	4.910	4.715	4.533
14	6.982	6.628	6.302	6.002	5.724	5.468	5.229	5.008	4.802	4.611
15	7.191	6.811	6.462	6.142	5.847	5.575	5.324	5.092	4.876	4.675
16	7.379	6.974	6.604	6.265	5.954	5.668	5.405	5.162	4.938	4.730
17	7.549	7.120	6.729	6.373	6.047	5.749	5.475	5.222	4.990	4.775
18	7.702	7.250	6.840	6.467	6.128	5.818	5.534	5.273	5.033	4.812
19	7.839	7.366	6.938	6.550	6.198	5.877	5.584	5.316	5.070	4.843
20	7.963	7.469	7.025	6.623	6.259	5.929	5.628	5.353	5.101	4.870

BPP
LEARNING MEDIA

Exam formulae

Valuation Models

(i)   Irredeemable preference share, paying a constant annual dividend, d, in perpetuity, where P_0 is the ex-div value:

$$P_0 = \frac{d}{k_{pref}}$$

(ii)   Ordinary (Equity) share, paying a constant annual dividend, d, in perpetuity, where P_0 is the ex-div value:

$$P_0 = \frac{d}{k_e}$$

(iii)   Ordinary (Equity) share, paying an annual dividend, d, growing in perpetuity at a constant rate, g, where P_0 is the ex-div value:

$$P_0 = \frac{d_1}{k_e - g} \text{ or } P_0 = \frac{d_0[1+g]}{k_e - g}$$

(iv)   Irredeemable (Undated) debt, paying annual after tax interest, $i\,(1-t)$, in perpetuity, where P_0 is the ex-interest value:

$$P_0 = \frac{i[1-t]}{k_{dnet}}$$

or, without tax:

$$P_0 = \frac{i}{k_d}$$

(v)   Future value of S, of a sum X, invested for n periods, compounded at $r\%$ interest:

$$S = X[1+r]^n$$

(vi)   Present value of £1 payable or receivable in n years, discounted at $r\%$ per annum:

$$PV = \frac{1}{[1+r]^n}$$

(vii)   Present value of an annuity of £1 per annum, receivable or payable for n years, commencing in one year, discounted at $r\%$ per annum:

$$PV = \frac{1}{r}\left[1 - \frac{1}{[1+r]^n}\right]$$

(viii)   Present value of £1 per annum, payable or receivable in perpetuity, commencing in one year, discounted at $r\%$ per annum:

$$PV = \frac{1}{r}$$

(ix) Present value of £1 per annum, receivable or payable, commencing in one year, growing in perpetuity at a constant rate of $g\%$ per annum, discounted at $r\%$ per annum:

$$PV = \frac{1}{r - g}$$

Cost of Capital

(i) Cost of irredeemable preference capital, paying an annual dividend, d, in perpetuity, and having a current ex-div price P_0:

$$k_{pref} = \frac{d}{P_0}$$

(ii) Cost of irredeemable debt capital, paying annual net interest, $i\,(1-t)$, and having a current ex-interest price P_0:

$$k_{dnet} = \frac{i[1-t]}{P_0}$$

(iii) Cost of ordinary (equity) share capital, paying an annual dividend, d, in perpetuity, and having a current ex-div price P_0:

$$k_e = \frac{d}{P_0}$$

(iv) Cost of ordinary (equity) share capital, having a current ex-div price, P_0, having just paid a dividend, d_0, with the dividend growing in perpetuity by a constant $g\%$ per annum:

$$k_e = \frac{d_1}{P_0} + g \quad \text{or} \quad k_e = \frac{d_0[1+g]}{P_0} + g$$

(v) Cost of ordinary (equity) share capital, using the CAPM:

$$k_e = R_f + [R_m - R_f]\beta$$

(vi) Weighted average cost of capital, k_0:

$$k_0 = k_e \left[\frac{V_E}{V_E + V_D}\right] + k_d \left[\frac{V_D}{V_E + V_D}\right]$$